NEW DIRECTIONS FOR PHILANTHROPIC FUNDRAISING

Timothy L. Seiler
The Center on Philanthropy at Indiana University

Cathlene Williams
Association of Fundraising Professionals
EDITORS

ACCOUNTABILITY:

A CHALLENGE FOR CHARITIES AND FUNDRAISERS

Putman Barber
The Evergreen State Society

EDITOR

NUMBER 31, SPRING 2001

ACCOUNTABILITY: A CHALLENGE FOR CHARITIES AND FUNDRAISERS
Putnam Barber (ed.)
New Directions for Philanthropic Fundraising, No. 31, Spring 2001
Timothy L. Seiler, Cathlene Williams, Editors

NEW DIRECTIONS FOR PHILANTHROPIC FUNDRAISING is indexed in Higher Education Abstracts and Philanthropic Index.

Microfilm copies of issues and articles are available in 16 mm and 35 mm, as well as microfiche in 105 mm, through University Microfilms Inc., 300 North Zeeb Road, Ann Arbor, Michigan 48106-1346.

ISSN 1072-172X ISBN 0-7879-4864-0

NEW DIRECTIONS FOR PHILANTHROPIC FUNDRAISING is part of the Jossey-Bass Nonprofit and Public Management Series and is published quarterly by Wiley Subscription Services, Inc., a Wiley company, at Jossey-Bass, 989 Market Street, San Francisco, California 94103-1741.

SUBSCRIPTIONS cost $75.00 for individuals and $147.00 for institutions, agencies, and libraries. Prices subject to change. Refer to the order form at the back of this issue.

EDITORIAL CORRESPONDENCE should be sent to Timothy L. Seiler, The Center on Philanthropy, Indiana University, 550 West North Street, Suite 301, Indianapolis, IN 46202-3162, or to Cathlene Williams, Association of Fundraising Professionals, 1101 King Street, Suite 700, Alexandria, VA 22314.

www.josseybass.com

Printed in the United States of America on acid-free recycled paper containing 100 percent recovered waste paper, of which at least 20 percent is postconsumer waste.

Contents

Editor's Notes

DONORS, OR AT LEAST some donors, fear that too much of their contributions to charities will be consumed by overhead and administration and too little will make its way to serving those in need, to addressing organizations' missions. This fear is an unfortunate but predictable consequence of the existence of charities that operate on a national or international scale and pursue complex goals and intractable problems with a wide variety of programs.

Efforts to ensure accountability—to provide evidence that charitable resources are focused on philanthropic ends or to reassure donors that their gifts are being well used—parallel the growth of the nonprofit sector in the United States. Early community chest organizations sought, among other goals, to impose management disciplines on the recipients of charitable social service funding. The National Charities Information Bureau was formed in response to concerns about the operations of the veterans' relief organizations that sought donations nationwide following World War I.

By the end of the twentieth century, pursuit of nonprofit accountability had led in several directions. Scholars and consultants had refined a variety of tools for nonprofit leaders to use in assessing the performance of their own organizations. Professional groups, nonprofit associations (often of organizations in a single field of service), and other voluntary organizations had developed procedures for review of nonprofits' finances and activities. In a few cases, accreditation undertaken by such groups can force drastic changes in an organization's work as a condition of continuing operation. Some forty state legislatures have created registration and reporting requirements for organizations that solicit financial support from their citizens. Congress has directed the Internal Revenue Service (IRS) to collect and publish information about recognized tax-exempt charities, and recently it imposed on every reporting charitable organization the duty of making this information available to the public.

At the very end of the twentieth century, these developments were complemented by a dramatic expansion of publicly accessible data about nonprofits on the World Wide Web. Nonprofits themselves created Web pages to provide services, distribute information about themselves and their work, and solicit donations and volunteers. In May 2001, for example, the Web search service Google (an intentional misspelling of the mathematicians' word for "a very large number") identified 1.45 million Web sites that included the word *nonprofit* or *charity.* The IRS rules about public disclosure of exempt organizations' information return (Form 990) were designed to encourage filers to post full copies of their recent submissions as well; many can now be viewed on-line.

Nonprofit managers, researchers, watchdog and accreditation organizations, state and federal officials, and Internet site operators collectively are committing a great deal of time and other resources to facilitating nonprofit accountability. But there is little agreement about whether these resources are adequate to the task or whether the underlying purposes are being achieved. Observers also disagree, and sometimes strongly, about what the next steps in the evolution of nonprofit accountability should be: greater reliance on government review, more detailed standards and gatekeeping, more active donor education coupled with dissemination of more and more timely information, or stronger sanctions against organizations that are found to be abusing the public's trust. There are some voices as well advancing the view that the current investments in accountability are misplaced—that the expense and uncertainty connected with trying to remain accountable detract from charities' ability to perform their key missions.

Why is nonprofit accountability important and difficult to achieve?

The chapters in this issue provide background on the development and the current state of various approaches to accountability. They will help fundraisers and others concerned with the future of America's nonprofits to join in discussions about future changes in mechanisms for accountability with greater knowledge and confidence.

Donors whose expectations are not met are often surprised to discover the narrow range of options they have for influencing the work of the organization they have supported. Evelyn Brody in Chapter One traces the origins of these principles and considers the choices donors have in structuring their gifts to increase the leverage they can exercise if the need arises.

In addition to the need to maintain general public confidence and the support of donors, nonprofit organizations are also subject to operating constraints and legal sanctions that arise from both their status as corporations and the specifics of laws dealing with nonprofit and tax-exempt entities. Geoffrey Peters in Chapter Two outlines the scope and impact of various federal laws affecting nonprofits, including the newly enacted intermediate sanctions, which punish managers, and not the damaged organizations, for some forms of misuse of exempt organizations' resources. He touches on the ways state governments can, and do, intervene to redirect the ways nonprofit organizations operate.

These two chapters show that most well-run nonprofits can expect to operate indefinitely without intervention by any external authority. The disclosure requirements imposed on exempt entities and on fundraising activities give leverage to attentive donors and other observers, including potential users of agencies' services. The possibility of adverse governmental action also encourages a cautious approach on the part of leaders and directors of nonprofits who are mindful of the lasting consequences of loss of confidence from their community of supporters.

What can nonprofits themselves do to improve accountability?

The nonprofit sector encompasses a vast number of small organizations at the base of a broad pyramid that peaks with a few institutions whose scale matches that of large for-profit enterprises. Maintaining internal controls and commitment to goals for the smaller organizations is often a matter of informal communications among stakeholders. But as the scale of operations increases, the challenges of internal accountability become difficult to meet, particularly because the character of charitable nonprofits' work cannot be neatly summarized by any single statistic. They do not have, in any meaningful sense of the term, a bottom line.

Analytical tools are available to approach this problem in ways that respect the special character of nonprofit enterprises. Vic Murray reviews several of them in Chapter Three. He concludes that individual enterprises can gain much from sustained use of one or another of the available methods of assembling meaningful data about operations and effectiveness. His review also confirms the great difficulties that face any effort to build measures of effectiveness that can guide comparative judgments among organizations, even in a narrowly defined field of service, much less report on the cumulative contribution of organizations considered as a group.

One state, Minnesota, is the focus of the work of an independent charity review organization, itself a nonprofit. Angela Bies describes the work of this forty-five-year-old group, the Charities Review Council, in her research reported in Chapter Four. The issue of whether to attempt determinations of organizational effectiveness, in addition to the operational measures addressed by current standards, has been the subject of recent discussions among the Charities Review Council, the organizations it examines, and other stakeholders. Consistent with the result of Murray's examinations of available tools, the conclusion of the discussions in Minnesota has been to maintain the current focus of the council's reviews. Managers and donors both report that the attention of the council to nonprofits' operations helps guide their decisions in useful ways and that this form of accountability helps to sustain the particularly vibrant nonprofit sector in the state.

Summary measures of the scope and character of the nonprofit sector warrant attention from many other perspectives in addition to the difficult dimension of effectiveness. Since the 1970s, the National Center for Charitable Statistics (NCCS) has been compiling data of interest to advocates, policymakers, social scientists, and other observers. Only recently have the data processing facilities caught up with the sheer volume of data already routinely collected. Thomas Pollak and Linda Lampkin sketch these developments in their discussion in Chapter Five of the work of NCCS. They describe the ways their own organization is collaborating with other nonprofits and government agencies to improve the quality of information about individual organizations and systematize the preparation of summary reports focused on the varied interests and concerns of observers of the sector. These efforts range from the development of taxonomies that can be employed by any administrator or researcher to structure the data to the preparation of software that will simplify the preparation of Form 990 in a consistent way.

What changes are on the regulatory horizon?

More than three-quarters of the states have established some registration and reporting requirements focused on organizations that solicit funds from the public in the name of charity. The terms vary from state to state, applying to or excluding different sorts of fundraising and reaching or exempting different groups of individuals and firms depending on the local legislative history and legal precedents. Daniel Moore describes in Chapter Six the recent discussion among the members of the National Association of State Charities Officials of ways to streamline and rationalize these requirements, particularly in the light of the changed patterns of communication that follow from increased use of the Internet by nonprofits for both delivering services and seeking financial support.

Sara Melendéz is president of INDEPENDENT SECTOR, the national umbrella group for charitable nonprofits. In Chapter Seven, she comments on recent calls for additional reporting by nonprofits and for disclosure of financial details that are kept confidential under current law. The measure of any such change, she urges, is that it should be addressed to a demonstrated need for further special treatment of nonprofit organizations and balance the burden of administrative expense against the benefits received by individuals and the community as a whole from access to more information.

Because much of the communication between donors and nonprofit organizations is the responsibility of fundraisers, the people who do that work play a central role in the way our society holds nonprofits accountable for the resources that are entrusted to them and the ways they work within the privileged environment afforded them by tax and other laws. In the midst of the daily pressures to ensure reliable support for critical community programs, a call to serve as the bearers of the burden of maintaining public confidence in the sector as a whole in addition to the work of one's own organization may seem unreasonable. Yet the chapters of this volume allow no other conclusion. It is the confidence of donors that sustains the precious donated funds that make it possible for nonprofits to achieve their missions. No one—neither donors nor nonprofit leaders—can expect any outside force to guarantee the continued strength of donors' faith or that nonprofits will continue to deserve the special confidence with which they are viewed. Government agencies and specialized monitoring organizations can patrol the periphery. The essential core, though, is in the care of those who do the daily work of nonprofit charities across the land, especially of those who represent nonprofits' needs for continuing support to the wider community of current and potential donors.

Putnam Barber
Editor

PUTNAM BARBER *is president of The Evergreen State Society in Seattle, Washington, and editor of the Internet Nonprofit Center.*

As illustrated by the recent controversy over the American Red Cross's handling of contributions for victims of the September 11 attacks, the legal rights of donors generally depend on state attorneys general for vindication. This chapter considers some "self-help" techniques that donors can employ, and considers forces other than formal laws that govern the charity-donor relationship.

1

Enforcement: Legal standing and private remedies

Evelyn Brody

THE ABSOLUTE DISCRETION of a donor to give or withhold making a charitable gift with whatever conditions the donor may see fit to impose is, to some, the essence of private philanthropy. Professionals who work with charities and donors struggle with finding proper boundaries for the involvement of donors, reflecting concerns that donor restrictions might violate a nonprofit's mission statement or conflicts-of-interest policy or even the requirement that it operate exclusively for the public benefit (Association of Fundraising Professionals, 2000). The charity also has the right not to accept the gift as restricted, of course, but we will assume here that the charity desires the gift.

Once a gift has been made or pledged, however, the arrangements could veer from plan. A charity might not use a contribution as the donor directed (or as the charity promised in soliciting the gift). A donor might not fulfill a pledge. Less simply, a charity might shift its initial mission, or it might maintain its mission but shift its methods of implementation, to the detriment of current beneficiaries.

Private philanthropy and the nonprofit sector rest on the fundamental constitutional guarantees not only of freedom of worship and expression, but also of private property and liberty of contract. However, applying property law and contract law concepts to public benefit activities raises difficult issues of legal enforcement. In theory, donor-imposed restrictions on charitable contributions are legally binding. In practice, generally only the state attorney general has standing to complain in court about a charity's activities, including its use of a restricted gift. Such a structure puts pressure on "the inclination and budget of a public official to vindicate [the beneficiaries'] rights" *Oberly v. Kirby*, 592 A.2d 445, 468 (Del. 1991). Even when a case reaches the courts, judges are far more likely to address fiduciary self-dealing and other breaches of loyalty than matters left to the business judgment of boards. Those who criticize the shortcomings of the current legal structure, though, should bear in mind that we are wrestling with the same dilemmas that prompted the 1601 Statute of Charitable Uses, another ineffective mechanism for enforcing charitable trusts (Brody, 1998).

Legal rights and obligations, however, make up only a subset of the forces that produce accountability in the nonprofit sector. Indeed, legal remedies constitute the least important part of charities' institutional landscape (Brody, 1996). This chapter first describes the legal powers of donors, then considers the legal structure for enforcing philanthropic promises and fiduciary obligations, and concludes with a brief discussion of private remedies.

Legal privileging of donor power

The charitable donor's authority to determine what to spend his money on and how is enshrined in Anglo-American law. Even today, as contributions fall as a percentage of charity receipts, the donor remains a privileged persona in the law. Nevertheless, as with other uses of wealth in the United States, some might believe that large donors have too much power over charity operations and small donors too little.

Donors face two fundamental difficulties in trying to control the use of their gifts: they can only imperfectly monitor the charity, and even if they can, they will not live forever. Accordingly, a variety of giving mechanisms and vehicles has developed to allow for increased donor control. At the most institutionalized level, a wealthy donor can establish a private foundation for making particularized grants, even into perpetuity, and attempt to staff the foundation with trusted confederates. Those donors having less wealth can often exercise some level of advice, if not formal control, through multiyear gifts, community foundations, and federated giving, notably the United Way. However, relying on the expertise of professional philanthropic managers then raises the inevitable question of who monitors the monitors.

The trend at all levels of giving seems to be toward increased donor determination. Building on the donor-directed movement at the United Way, we now have what has become known as venture philanthropy, with its hands-on investment-like approach, and commercial donor-advised funds, such as the Fidelity Investments Charitable Gift Fund. In self-defense, community foundations and even individual public charities such as universities are beginning to offer donor-advised funds; these arrangements usually require a portion of annual giving to go to the host institution. Obviously, as donor control increases, the benefits of a professional, centralized identification of needs and allocation of resources offered by intermediaries diminish.

Under charitable trust law, the wishes of the donor determine the use of the gift forever. Even if the charity takes the corporate rather than the trust form, it must honor restrictions placed on a gift. Of course, no mortal has perfect foresight. If it subsequently becomes impossible to carry out the specified charitable purpose, the legal doctrine of *cy pres* permits the trustees (with court approval) to apply the assets to another purpose as close as possible to the one originally designated. However, under current law, no attempt is made to determine whether a different charitable purpose would be more socially useful or effective. (A general Uniform Trust Code was approved in August 2000 by the National Conference of Commissioners on Uniform State Laws, and time will tell whether states adopt it; Section 413 would also allow *cy pres* where the donor's purpose becomes "impracticable" or "wasteful.") Some believe that this notion of donor control also extends in a parallel way to the wishes of the incorporators of a corporate charity. That is, directors might owe a duty of obedience to the original mission of the organization as stated in its articles of incorporation, and some courts have applied quasi–*cy pres* principles to nonprofit corporate charities.

The inherently conservative nature of the legal structure is controversial (Brody, 1997). Rule by the "dead hand" pleases those who fear the prospect of unfettered discretion by current trustees and frustrates those who believe, like Jefferson, that "the land belongs to the living." This focus on donor dictate so permeates the legal regulation of charities that it can infringe on charity fiduciaries' ability to govern. As a practical matter, the issue rarely becomes serious, because most charities are formed with missions broad enough to accommodate evolving needs, and narrowly restricted gifts do not usually constitute so large a percentage of a charity's assets as to prevent rational decision making. The real battles occur when other stakeholders, such as students, foundation grantees, or beneficiaries, seek to influence the institution within the confines of its purposes.

Legal remedies for breach

A charity that breaches conditions placed on a gift can be sued, but the question is, By whom? U.S. law generally allows only the state attorney general to sue on behalf of the charity's indefinite beneficiaries for misapplication of the contribution. Despite the legal veneration of the donor, the donor *merely as donor* has no standing to challenge the charity's use of a restricted gift. In essence, donors (like beneficiaries) are just members of the public, and the public has no standing to sue for breach of charitable trust. From the other side of the transaction, in certain circumstances a charity can sue a donor who has promised to make a contribution but fails to follow through.

Breach by the charity

Standing is a jurisdictional prerequisite to a plaintiff's bringing a legal action. For our purposes, the concept requires the plaintiff to have a sufficient and particularized interest in the outcome of the action to ensure that the plaintiff makes the proper arguments. Moreover, the law has long sought to minimize the risk of vexatious and multiple lawsuits against charities in order to preserve charitable assets that would otherwise pay for defense. Accordingly, members of the general public lack standing to complain about wrongs done by or to charities. Moreover, in the absence of a state statute to the contrary, suit cannot be brought by donors or beneficiaries, and few charities have members with the type of authority that would give them standing. The standing requirement also allows the courts to avoid disputes committed to another branch of government. Thus, a taxpayer as such has no standing to complain about the tax exemption that Congress granted to a given class of charities or about the decision of the Internal Revenue Service (IRS) not to seek revocation of a particular charity's exemption.

Distinguishing between direct actions and derivative actions helps us to see when standing is appropriate. In a direct action, the plaintiff seeks to enforce his or her own rights, and any monetary recovery would generally go to the plaintiff. By contrast, a plaintiff's rights in a derivative suit derive from the rights of the charity, and any monetary recovery would go to the charity. Why wouldn't the charity bring its own lawsuit against those who have harmed it? The problem arises when the charity's very trustees, directors, or officers are alleged to have breached their fiduciary duties of loyalty or care, and the majority of trustees or directors refuse to sue.

Derivative suits are common in the business world, but are not universally recognized under state nonprofit laws. In every state, though, under the common law and modern nonprofit statutes, the state attorney general has standing to sue wayward fiduciaries.

For example, assume a donor made a gift to Alma Mater University, the income from which is to be used for the school of nursing; the gift document provides, however, that should Alma Mater cease teaching nursing, the principal is to be returned to the donor. Years later, Alma Mater decides to close its nursing school. If it refuses to return the donor's gift, she (or her estate or heirs, depending on how much time has passed) can bring a direct action to recover the amount. For many reasons, including the fear of jeopardizing the tax deduction, this is a rare arrangement; gifts are typically irrevocable.

By contrast, consider the same gift without a right of reversion. Once Alma Mater closes its nursing school, it must make alternate plans for the restricted gift, but there is no question that the funds remain with the institution. Assume the school decides to use the income for medical school scholarships. If the donor is still alive and agrees to this change in use and if the state is one of forty-seven that has adopted the Uniform Management of Institutional Funds Act (UMIFA), the parties can privately alter the restriction. If, however, the donor believes the funds should instead be used for indigent care at the university hospital and so refuses to consent but the school alters the use anyway, then what happens? In a similar case, the Connecticut Supreme Court held that UMIFA did not give the donor standing to bring a lawsuit. *Carl J. Herzog Foundation, Inc.* v. *University of Bridgeport*, 699 A.2d 995 (Conn. 1997). The donor does not have standing under common law either because the issue is how the organization will use its funds, not whether the donor should get them back.

A technique exists to avoid this problem. Assume that instead of providing for a reversion, the gift document provides for a "gift over" to an alternate charity if Alma Mater does not or cannot use the funds as directed. The alternate charity now has a direct interest in monitoring the initial donee's use of the funds, and it has standing to sue to enforce its rights. (Although not all state laws require the first charity to notify the second of its contingent rights, a donor who drafts a "gift over" for this purpose will be sure to provide a copy of the gift document to the second charity.) Unfortunately, this technique does not allow the initial donee to keep the funds where the change in use is not its fault.[1]

A few modern statutes grant standing to an expanded class of private persons. California permits any of the following to "bring an action to enjoin, correct, obtain damages for or to otherwise remedy a breach of a charitable trust": the corporation; a member; an officer; a director; a person with a reversionary, contractual, or property interest in the assets subject to such charitable trust; and the attorney general or any person granted "relator" status by the attorney general. (A relator is a party permitted to bring suit in the name of the people where the attorney general has exclusive legal authority; the practice is not widespread because of a variety of restrictions.) The attorney general must be given notice of any action brought by the other persons specified and may intervene (Cal. Corp. Code § 5142 (a)). "In a suit by a relator, the relator generally takes an active part in the proceeding and is responsible for court costs, but the attorney general retains control of the action and can withdraw, dismiss or compromise it at any time" (Blasko, Crossley, and Lloyd, 1993, p. 49; Fishman, 1985, p. 674).

New York grants standing in suits for breach of fiduciary duty to the attorney general and to the corporation; a director or officer; members holding 5 percent of voting power; and, if the certificate of incorporation or the bylaws so provide, to any contributor of at least $1,000. The 1987 Revised Model Nonprofit Corporation Act, drafted by the American Bar Association and adopted in several states, permits derivative suits by any director, as well as by fifty members (or, if fewer, members having 5 percent of the vote). Notice must be given to the attorney general, who has the right to join in the action, and the court has discretion to award expenses (including attorney's fees) on finding that the suit was commenced without reasonable cause. (In all of these cases, the term *member* means someone with the authority to vote for the board.) In addition, courts on rare occasion will grant standing to those with a special interest.

Neither courts nor legislature, however, show signs of more broadly liberalizing the standing rules. The Massachusetts Supreme Court recently held that mere membership in the Christian Science church or other public charity was not enough to allow standing to contest mismanagement (*Weaver* v. *Wood,* 680 N.E.2d 918 (Mass. 1997), *cert. denied* 522 U.S. 1049 (1998). The Connecticut Supreme Court ruled that a nonvoting "life trustee" had no standing, either as a director or as someone with a special interest, to challenge the University of Bridgeport's decision to affiliate with a school founded by the Reverend Sun Myung Moon (*Steeneck* v. *University of Bridgeport,* 1996). The same court also ruled against donor standing under UMIFA. Section 405(c) of the new Uniform Trust Code would allow the creator "of a charitable trust . . . [to] maintain a proceeding to enforce the trust," but this model statute has not yet been adopted in any state. In 2000, at the request of the attorney general, the New York legislature considered granting standing to a donor to sue for breach of a restriction on a gift, but only upon notice to the attorney general—and if a court determined that the suit was frivolous, it could award attorneys' fees to the charity (Senate Bill 7805). The New York attorney general did not seek reintroduction of this bill, purportedly in light of a recent appellate court decision expanding standing (Josephson, 2001, at note 11).[2]

A charity that accepts restricted gifts (or raises funds for specific, identified purposes) should take steps to ensure that its staff members are aware of their obligations and adhere to specified requirements. One excellent guide suggests that the charity maintain a list of the contact information for the donors and their key relatives to facilitate UMIFA relief. The authors also suggest that the charity work with donors in setting forth appropriately flexible language in the gift documents. In addition, where an older institution "has a large number of restricted funds that tend, over time, to become underutilized," it "should have an ongoing review process to identify such funds and seek modification of the terms of the trust to make the funds productive on a current basis" (Peregrine and Schwartz, 2000, p. 34). A charity might informally consult with the state attorney general's office for guidance—and to forestall a suit for breach of fiduciary duty. Ultimately, court relief may be necessary.

Breach by the donor

From the other side, what happens when donors fail to perform as promised? Under traditional contract law, in the ordinary case, the charity has provided no reciprocal consideration to the donor. Nevertheless, courts in most states will enforce a pledge or installment gift if the charity has relied on the donor's promise to its detriment or if the promise induced others to give. (Assume that none of the other contract defenses apply—that is, assume the donor had the mental capacity to make the gift, and the charity did not apply fraud, undue influence, or duress.) We are starting to see lawsuits by charities against donors who default on their (major) pledges, often when the donor dies and the will makes no mention of the promise.

Charities seem uneasy about their rights and obligations in such a case, worried about the bad publicity and its effects on prospective donors (Butig, Butler, and Murphy, 1992). Some charities worry that they *must* sue because of the accounting rules that required them to book the pledge when made (Strosnider, 1998). Although the law does not impose such an obligation, a board that fails to consider the benefits as well as the costs of suing has not exercised its duty of care. As a practical matter, according to a recent study, "accounting practices and nonprofit pledge management policies have made pledging an increasingly less frequent gift vehicle" (Briscoe and Marion, 2000).

As a separate matter, when must a charity return a gift? When may it? Does it matter whether a crime is the source of the donated funds?[3] As in many areas of philanthropy, legal practice is guided more by professional judgment than by precedent. Despite the reluctance of charities to make gifts look too contractual, every major pledge and installment gift should be formalized by a writing signed by both parties, and set out a clear payment schedule and a description of any other bargained-for conditions. The charity should keep a record of all activities undertaken in reliance on the donor's promise. And excessively cautious charities need to recognize that if they fail to sue where prudent, they can run the opposite risk of offending those donors who did follow through on their gifts.

Private "regulation"

In addition to the legal doctrines and practices, private mechanisms exist that shape the relationships between donors and charities. Disclosure of key information and review of such information by third parties has been increasing in recent years. Peer regulation and accreditation also provide monitoring and oversight in a more systematic way than any single donor might achieve.

Disclosure

A charitable contribution is a voluntary transaction. Donors who care about the use of their funds can withhold gifts if the potential donee is not forthcoming with requested information. Until recently, this power was confined to large donors as a practical matter. Small donors rarely found it worth the time and trouble to make detailed demands on charities which they were considering supporting, although charity watchdogs like the Better Business Bureau's Philanthropic Advisory Service, which recently merged with the National Charities Information Bureau into a new entity called the BBB Wise Giving Alliance, would respond to inquiries about whether specific charities met their guidelines.

Recent technological and legislative changes have drastically reduced the transaction costs of small (and not so small) donors who want to research specific charities. The privately funded project by GuideStar and the Urban Institute to provide financial information on individual charities was bolstered by Congress's requirement that charities produce their Form 990 on demand. Every filing charity should assume that its tax return information is instantly available for all the world on the Web—if not now, then soon. State charities officials might even be able to eliminate additional filings by charities whose financial information is available on the Internet. (See Chapter Six, this volume.)

This discussion assumes that donors care about how effectively the charity uses the funds—what I call instrumental giving. Giving can also occur for other (or additional) reasons, such as identification with a group, erection of a building, maintenance of wealth, or other expressive purpose. Now that disclosure is becoming widespread, we should be able to learn more about the extent to which donors care about the financial position of potential donees. In particular, we can see whether charities with large endowments and other surpluses will change their practices in order to continue attracting contributions. To pick a conspicuous example, Harvard University is careful to explain why, in spite of its enormous endowment, it still needs contributions (Harvard University, 2001).

Nevertheless, we still have a long way to go in terms of both voluntary (as opposed to third-party) disclosure and accuracy. An unscientific check of the Web sites of major charities reveals that few post any detailed information about their finances, activities, and plans. A commendable example is set by Care International, which posts both its annual report (complete with financial statements) and its Form 990. However, a visitor to this site who is concerned about the high ratio of assets to annual expenditures would not find any explanation for the charity's savings policy beyond a statement about that portion of assets held outside its control. A lamentable example is set by the Ohio Division of the American Cancer Society, which was rocked by the recent disclosure that a top official almost succeeded in embezzling more than $7 million; no mention of this serious breach of trust appears on the division's Web site. An editorial in the *Columbus Dispatch* scoffed at claims that the losses would be covered by insurance: "You cannot buy a policy that will insure against loss of public confidence" ("A Cancer Within: Crime Against Charity," 2000, p. 2B).

Codes of conduct and peer regulation

Private regulation takes many forms, which vary in their degree of voluntariness or compulsion and attendant sanction: at the individual organization level, the demands of institutional or government contract funders; at the industry or professional level, the requirements of accreditation bodies; and at the sector level, trade association best practices guides and even certification (see Brody, forthcoming).

Nonprofit watchdogs and associations have recently been designing accountability codes and standards of practice. Two of the most thorough, adopted in substantially identical form by the Maryland Association of Nonprofit Organizations and the Minnesota Council of Nonprofits, cover mission and program evaluation, governance, human resources, financial management, fundraising, public accountability and communications, and public policy and advocacy. Detailed enough to give specific guidance to directors who are usually volunteers, these documents provide useful examples of best practices. Finally, the Maryland association offers peer review certification for nonprofits seeking to demonstrate that they abide by its principles (see Figure 4.2).

Private regulation has advantages and disadvantages compared with the compulsory, but minimal, public regulation. A charity has some discretion in orienting itself toward particular types of validating private authorities with varying levels of requirements. A member-funded private body generally relies on voluntarily supplied and unverified information. Nevertheless, standards could be inappropriate in a given case, and a proliferation of different tests could either unnecessarily burden compliant charities or cause small charities lacking the sophistication or resources to conform to appear unworthy of donor support. The relationship between the private regulator and regulated can become just as complicated as in the public sector, with concerns of "capture" and protection of elite, vested interests (Meek, 1977, pp. 2842–2844). The real test of the effectiveness of private regulation comes when the nonprofit body expels nonconforming nonprofits or imposes other sanctions. Once again, regulation can merely move the "who guards the guardians" question one step up.[4]

Conclusion

Legally, except in rare cases, only the attorney general can call a charity to account, and rarely does the attorney general act. As a practical and political matter, though, charities must be responsive to their various stakeholders and the public at large. Today's charities face competition from a myriad of other charities, as well as high fundraising and administrative costs. Charities, when they are reluctant to release information that the public will misunderstand, or misinterpret, can appear secretive and dissembling. A public whose oversight, out of ignorance, focuses on the wrong considerations induces charities to adopt inefficient and ineffective behaviors. At the same time, charities face the difficulties of effectively absorbing the massive transfer wealth that is occurring. The head of Philanthropy Roundtable recently testified, "We know that waste, fraud, and abuse are the great dangers when large sums of money are poured into an area over a relatively short period" (Walters, 2001).

To address unrealistic expectations, individual organizations and the sector as a whole should improve their own as well as the public's understanding of charities' cost constraints, capacities, and program limitations. As suggested by a recent study by the staff of the congressional Joint Committee on Taxation (2000), even a charity totally self-sufficient on income from the performance of services and endowment cannot necessarily keep its activities to itself. An informed public should be a sympathetic public.

Notes

1. Perhaps the gift document could use language that says, "To Charity A for X purpose, but if Charity A cannot use the gift for X purpose *or obtain cy pres relief to reform the purpose,* then to Charity B." Nevertheless, it would be

difficult to restrict the "gift over" to cases where the primary charity failed to honor the gift, either willfully or by neglect.

2. To the surprise and strong criticism of legal scholars, an appellate court in New York recently granted standing to a donor's widow—as a court-appointed representative of her husband's estate—to challenge the use of his restricted gift, even though the attorney general had approved an alternate arrangement. Smithers v. St.Luke's-Roosevelt Hospital Center, 723 N.Y.S.2d 426 (App. Div. 2001). The three-judge majority opinion declared, "We conclude that the distinct but related interests of the donor and the Attorney General are best served by continuing to accord standing to donors to enforce the terms of their own gifts concurrent with the Attorney General's standing to enforce such gifts on behalf of the beneficiaries thereof." The lone dissenting judge provided a clear summary of the standing rules as they were previously understood, distinguishing between any rights that might be held by the donor, the donor's estate, and the donor's heirs.

3. Recall the Ponzi scheme run by the Foundation for New Era Philanthropy, which promised charities that if they deposited funds with the Foundation for six months, the money would be returned doubled by anonymous donors (who turned out not to exist). Hundreds of the early-participating organizations that benefited from the scheme agreed—some reluctantly—to pay $41 million to reimburse those that lost money. As a separate matter, Congress enacted the Religious Liberty and Charitable Donation Protection Act of 1998 (S. 1244) to protect tithing and charitable giving from the reach of creditors and bankruptcy trustees in a bankruptcy proceeding. Among other provisions, a voidable "fraudulent transfer" now excludes a "transfer of a charitable contribution to a qualified religious or charitable entity or organization . . . in any case in which—(A) the amount of that contribution does not exceed 15 percent of the gross annual income of the debtor for the year in which the transfer of the contribution is made; or (B) [a contribution was made in a greater percentage] . . . if the transfer was reasonable and consistent with the practices of the debtor in making charitable contributions."

4. Another form of private regulation could come from the insurance industry. Currently, directors-and-officers policies for nonprofit organizations come quite cheap and easily. However, after a few more $25 million payouts like the one made by the insurer of the Kamehameha Schools/Bishop Estate in Hawaii (see Greene, 2000), insurance companies might begin engaging in underwriting the risk of different types of nonprofit governance structures.

References

Association of Fundraising Professionals. "How Much Donor Involvement Is Too Much?", 2000. Available at http://www.nsfre.org/ethics (excerpted from *Advancing Philanthropy*, November/December, 2000).

Blasko, M. G., Crossley, C. S., and Lloyd, D. "Standing to Sue in the Charitable Sector." *University of San Francisco Law Review*, 1993, *28*, 37–84.

Briscoe, M. G., and Marion, B. H. "Capital Campaigns and the New Charitable Investors." In E. R. Tempel (ed.), *Changing Relations Between Donors and Organizations.* New Directions for Philanthropic Fundraising, no. 29. San Francisco: Jossey-Bass, 2000.

Brody, E. "Institutional Dissonance in the Nonprofit Sector." *Villanova Law Review*, 1996, *41*, 433–504.

Brody, E. "Charitable Endowments and the Democratization of Dynasty." *Arizona Law Review*, 1997, *39*, 873–948.

Brody, E. "The Limits of Charity Fiduciary Law." *Maryland Law Review*, 1998, *57*, 1400–1501.

Brody, E. "Accountability and Public Trust." In L. B. Salamon (ed.), *The State of America's Nonprofit Sector.* Washington, D.C.: Brookings Institution Press and The Aspen Institute, forthcoming.

Butig, M. F., Butler, G. T., and Murphy, L. M. "Pledges to Nonprofit Organizations: Are They Enforceable and Must They Be Enforced?" *University of San Francisco Law Review*, 1992, *27*, 47–147.

"A Cancer Within: Crime Against Charity Will Leave Deep Scars." *Columbus Dispatch*, June 11, 2000, p 2B.

Carl J. Herzog Foundation, Inc. v. University of Bridgeport, 699 A.2d 995 (Conn. 1997).

Fishman, J. J. "The Development of Nonprofit Corporation Law and an Agenda for Reform." *Emory Law Journal*, 1985, *34*, 617–683.

Greene, S. G. "Insurer to Pay $25 Million to Settle Dispute in Hawaii." *Chronicle of Philanthropy*, Oct. 5, 2000.

The Harvard Guide: Finances. 2001. http://www.news.harvard.edu/guide/finance/index.html.

Josephson, William. "Guiding Practitioners and Fiduciaries on Charities." New York Law Journal, Dec. 3, 2001. *Outside Counsel*, 1.

Meek, P. G. "Self-Regulation in Private Philanthropy." In *Commission on Private Philanthropy and Public Needs*, Vol. 5: 2781–2855. Washington, D.C.: U.S. Treasury Department, 1977.

Peregrine, M. W., and Schwartz, J. R. "A General Counsel's Guide to Accessing Restricted Gifts." *Exempt Organization Tax Review*, 2000, *29*, 27–34.

Strosnider, K. "Colleges Face Prickly Dilemma When Donors or Their Heirs Renege on Promised Gifts." *Chronicle of Higher Education*, June 26, 1998, p. A35.

U.S. Congress. Joint Committee on Taxation. *Study of Present-Law Taxpayer Confidentiality and Disclosure Provisions as Required by Section 3802 of the Internal Revenue Service Restructuring and Reform Act of 1998*, Vol. II: *Study of Disclosure Provisions Relating to Exempt Organizations.* Washington, D.C.: U.S. Government Printing Office, Jan. 28, 2000. http://www.house.gov/jct. Harvard University.

Walters, J. P. "Testimony of John P. Walters, President of the Philanthropy Roundtable Before the Committee on Finance, United States Senate." March 14, 2001. Available in LEXIS, Fedtax Library, Tax Notes Today File, as 2001 TNT 51–65 (Mar. 15, 2001).

EVELYN BRODY *is professor of law at Chicago-Kent College of Law, Illinois Institute of Technology.*

What happens when voluntary accountability fails? Who is responsible, what are the consequences and what institutions seek to bring those consequences to bear? This brief synopsis attempts to outline the answers to those questions under the American legal system.

2

By what means? Accountability and the law

Geoffrey Peters

WHO IS RESPONSIBLE and therefore ultimately accountable for nonprofit organizations? Is it the board members as they exercise their fiduciary responsibilities? Nonprofit executives acting as proper stewards? Donors who may choose to give money or withhold it? Voluntary watchdog groups? Or government officials, who presumably represent the general public? Arguably, all of these have a role to play. But what are those roles, and what happens when one or another group does not play them properly?

It seems clear that the ultimate control over nonprofits rests with donors. They can, by giving or withholding money or other resources, exercise the blunt instrument of financial control. The decision to grant funds, whether by a foundation board or a major giver or the individual donor who puts ten dollars in an envelope and mails it to the nonprofit, is the ultimate expression of belief or lack thereof in the mission and performance of the grantee.

What if the resources have already been granted and are now being wastefully or inappropriately employed? Clearly, nonprofit executives have an immediate fiduciary duty to donors and perhaps the public, as well as a duty as employees to the organization. If these executives were doing their jobs properly, perhaps the waste, fraud, or abuse would not be occurring. And although they may be primarily responsible as employees, they have supervisors—that is, the nonprofit's board of directors—who have a greater responsibility and broader fiduciary duty. This point has been made often. One early statement of the principle comes from the Ohio Supreme Court: "It is well established that a corporation officer occupies a position of trust in relation to his corporation. . . . Such relationship imposes upon directors duties in the nature of a fiduciary obligation" (*Thomas* v. *Matthews*, 1916).

The Board of Directors or Trustees

It seems commonly conceded that the last, best opportunity (short of intervention by the government) to rectify problems in the operation of nonprofits rests with their governing boards. Yet persistent expert commentary and anecdotal evidence suggest that this is where the failure of accountability most often occurs (Covington, 1994).

One of the most responsible and responsive watchdog organizations (and one that nearly uniquely operates under principles of providing assistance in addition to review and accreditation) is the Evangelical Council for Financial Accountability. Having undertaken field accreditation reviews of literally scores of nonprofit organizations, it has had time to hone its standards, determine where problems most often lie, and provide an objective evaluation of the possible threats or sources of difficulty for nonprofits with which they work. The issue it finds most significant when conducting field reviews is board governance (Evangelical Council, 2000). Its own standards commentary says, "Virtually every not-for-profit organization that has encountered failure or even worse, scandal, can trace its difficulties to some breakdown at the Board level" (Evangelical Council, 2000, p. 1).

To be sure there are others that can play a role in this process:

> Some full boards, finance and/or audit committees monitor themselves with the assistance of outside financial advisors; and some chief executives or chief financial officers take the lead in alerting their boards to financial crisis. Voluntary accrediting organizations and many different state and federal agencies monitor schools and colleges. Government funding agencies monitor the groups to which they give grants or contracts. Some national organizations monitor their local affiliates. Some local umbrella funding organizations, such as United Way or Jewish Federation, monitor their grantees. Some lending institutions or insurance companies monitor groups which apply for loans or insurance [Evangelical Council, 2000, p. 3].

Other watchdog agencies, such as the Wise Giving Alliance (formerly Philanthropic Advisory Service) of the Council of Better Business Bureaus Foundation, monitor nonprofits on behalf of donors and play a comparatively minor role in alerting boards to problems of financial viability (Bograd, 1995; Better Business Bureau, 2001). Nevertheless, it is with the board of directors that the buck stops. It should not be surprising that while others may be drawn into the debate, many of the legal sanctions that give teeth to accountability apply to the board. What follows is a brief review of some of the legal sanctions that can be imposed as a result of failures of accountability.

Federal legal sanctions

A number of federal agencies have the ability to intervene in the event of a failure of accountability in nonprofit organizations. For example, the U.S. Postal Service gains a role because of its special or nonprofit bulk third-class rate. A rule known as the "cooperative mailing rule" that has been the subject of much criticism and litigation forbids the use of the nonprofit mail permit when there is an appearance that for-profit organizations might benefit from the mailing (U.S. Postal Service, 1996). The postal service also has authority, along with U.S. attorneys throughout the United States, to enforce statutes against mail fraud. Congress has specifically empowered the postal service to rid the U.S. mails of matter sent to further a scheme or device for obtaining money or property by false representations. If the postal service determines that a person is engaging in fraudulent activity through the use of the mails or is receiving funds under false pretenses, it may initiate an investigation and take administrative action against the offending person, culminating in the entry of an order that directs the postmaster to return to the sender mail addressed to the offending person, forbids the payment by the postmaster of money orders made out to the offending person, and requires the offending person to cease and desist from engaging in any such scheme (39 U.S.C. § 3005(a); 39 C.F.R. Part 952).

Furthermore, U.S. attorneys also have the authority to enforce general violations of federal criminal law, which includes offenses involving interstate commerce. Antitrust law may apply to nonprofit organizations. The American Medical Association, for example, was held to have engaged in an illegal boycott of chiropractors (*Wilk* v. *American Medical Association*, 1990). Efforts to restrict competition, for example, in the medical services field or cooperation among Ivy League schools in giving financial aid, can be actionable under the antitrust laws (*Key Enterprises of Delaware* v. *Venice Hospital*, 1990; Smith, 1990). Federal election laws, however, may not apply to nonprofits under certain circumstances (*Federal Election Commission* v. *Massachusetts Citizens for Life*, 1986). State or federal statutes may properly limit political expenditures of funds by nonprofit organizations, and these limitations may be enforced administratively by the Internal Revenue Service (IRS) and state officials, as well as by judicial action (*Austin* v. *Michigan Chamber of Commerce*, 1990; 26 United States Code 501 (c)(3)).

Perhaps the broadest federal power to impose sanctions on nonprofit organizations is held by the IRS, which can, among other penalties, revoke tax-exempt status as well as deny tax deductibility to donations. Such revocations can occur not only over what might be viewed as narrow and technical failures of accountability but also because the organization is, in the view of the IRS, failing to act in accordance with broad public policy and therefore is no longer operating in the public interest.

For example, in *Bob Jones University* v. *United States* (1983), the U.S. Supreme Court held that racial discrimination in education is against public policy and that the IRS is empowered to make that determination. As a result, the university was denied recognition as "charitable" under the Internal Revenue Code, which means, among other things, that donors to it cannot deduct their gifts from their personal income taxes.

This is a case where the very nature of the organization, and not merely some dealings the organization had with others, was questioned. The case is not unique. In a tax court case later affirmed by the Ninth Circuit Court of Appeals, *Church of Scientology of California* v. *Commissioner* (1987), it was held that the church violated public policy because, in violation of federal criminal laws, its actions had interfered with the collection of federal taxes it owed. Its tax exemption was revoked.

In addition, the IRS has on numerous occasions held unpaid volunteers such as directors personally liable if the nonprofit has failed to withhold federal income and social security taxes properly. Imagine being a volunteer director of a local community nonprofit hospital and finding your personal assets attached because the hospital's accounting department failed to pay hundreds of thousands of dollars of withholding taxes on its employees (26 U.S.C. § 6672).

The Internal Revenue Code also requires that nonprofits make available for public inspection and copying both their application for tax exemption and their three most recent annual information returns (known as Form 990). The nonprofit may comply with these disclosure requirements by posting downloadable copies of its forms on a publicly accessible Web site. These provisions were included in the 1996 "Taxpayer Bill of Rights" (Public Law 104(168) to facilitate public scrutiny of the financial affairs and other business practices of tax-exempt organizations. They were at least in part a reaction to a widespread perception that nonprofits had made accessing this information more difficult than necessary under the previous standard of voluntary distribution.

Recently, the IRS asked Congress for authority to impose less stringent consequences when nonprofits commit violations so that it could avoid the binary choice between no sanctions on one extreme and what has sometimes been referred to as the "death penalty" for nonprofits (revocation of tax exempt status) on the other. Since passage of the Taxpayer Bill of Rights, what has become known as intermediate sanctions is found in section 4958 of the Internal Revenue Code. That section provides that the sanctions apply to excess benefit transactions, which are defined as transactions where a disqualified person receives a more than fair market economic benefit from an organization exempt from taxes under section 501(c)(3) or (4). This includes nearly all charitable organizations except private foundations.

Lloyd Mayer of the law firm Caplin & Drysdale described these intermediate sanctions by writing that the law

> imposes a tax, equal to 10% of the excess benefit, on any organization manager who knowingly participated in the excess benefit transaction, unless the participation was not willful and was due to reasonable cause.
>
> The tax is imposed on an organization manager only if the manager (1) had actual knowledge of sufficient facts to determine that the transaction would be an excess benefit transaction; (2) was aware that the act might violate the federal tax law governing excess benefit transactions; and (3) either negligently failed to make reasonable attempts to ascertain whether the transaction was an excess benefit transaction or knew that the transaction was an excess benefit transaction (Mayer, 1998).

An organization manager includes specifically members of its board of directors or trustees or any individuals having similar responsibilities. Thus, directors become ultimately and personally accountable for such transactions.

The intermediate sanctions legislation is getting a lot of attention by IRS enforcement officials, according to the nonprofit trade press. One account reports that documents filed in the tax court show that

> the Internal Revenue Service has assessed more than $40 million in intermediate sanctions excise taxes against one individual who was an officer and director in several nonprofit home health agencies that converted from nonprofit to for-profit status. The IRS also proposed revoking the agencies' tax-exempt status retroactively.
>
> In these cases, several related individuals caused the assets of the agencies to be transferred to newly-created for-profit entities, all of which the

individuals controlled. Consideration for the transfer was the corporations' assumption of liabilities of the nonprofit entities. The shareholders secured a valuation opinion that the assumption of liabilities represented "fair market value" for the assets transferred. The Service disagreed, based on appraisals conducted by its own valuation personnel, and assessed intermediate sanctions taxes on the individuals and entities involved.

The litigation makes clear that the IRS will use its new enforcement tools vigorously, a fact that is underlined by a key Service official's statement that intermediate sanctions will be a "very live issue" with revenue agents in 2000 [McGovern, 2000].

Violations of the statute and regulations can include inappropriate conflicts of interest and failure of the board of directors to review compensation and financial transactions involving officers or other "disqualified persons" in the light of objective data such as comparative salary and benefits studies and to document that such studies were consulted and properly applied (Wright, 1997).

The Federal Trade Commission (FTC) might also be included in the list of federal agencies charged with maintaining nonprofit standards of behavior. Until 2001 it had no distinct jurisdiction over nonprofits and thus its regulatory activities, including enforcement of the Telephone Sales Act and other FTC rules and regulations either implicitly or explicitly exempted nonprofits. However Section 1011 of HR 3162 (USA Patriot Act) amending 15 USC §6102 (telemarketing rules) suddenly and recently changed that. The FTC's jurisdiction is extended by this act to include "fraudulent charitable solicitations" and solicitors are required to disclose that their purpose in calling is "to solicit charitable contributions, donations, or gifts."

State legal sanctions

At the state government level, the situation is murkier. Some state statutes provide for immunity for volunteer board members or trustees, but there are also criminal statutes that can be violated by any participants in questionable transactions. Volunteer board members or trustees may, in addition, seek indemnity or insurance from a nonprofit organization to protect them. Available protections are likely to come from the nonprofit's directors-and-officers liability policy. In many cases, such policies will not cover employment issues such as race or sex discrimination or harassment or suits brought by the attorney general or the IRS seeking to hold board members personally liable for their personal improper conduct or that of other board members in conflict-of-interest and other situations. A number of state statutes and state constitutional provisions provide for the attorneys general of various states to act on behalf of the public to ensure the operation of charities in the public interest.

Situations that might call for federal intermediate sanctions can cause state supervisory organizations to become involved. For example, as a result of a petition filed by some faculty, students, and former members of Adelphi University's board of trustees charging the current board of trustees with neglect of duty and misconduct,

> the New York State Board of Regents decided that the Board of Trustees of Adelphi University was guilty of neglect of duty and misconduct in connection with certain conflict of interest transactions. . . . The Attorney General in the Adelphi case made it clear that the Board Members may be held personally liable for their own as well as the misconduct of their fellow Board Members [Atnally, 1998, p. 70].

The Supreme Court recognized this power many years ago when it approved the taking of property of the Mormon church because of its espousal of polygamy:

> Chancellor James Kent [first professor of law at Columbia College, from 1793] says: "In this country, the legislature or government of the state, as parens patriae, has the right to enforce all charities of a public nature, by virtue of its general superintending authority over the public interests, where no other person is in trusted with it" (4 Kent, Comm. 508, note). (See http://www.kentlaw.edu/perritt/chancellor.html). In *Fontain* v. *Ravenel,* (17 How. 369, 384) Mr. Justice McLean, delivering the opinion of this court in a charity case, said: "When this country achieved its independence, the prerogatives of the crown devolved upon the people of the states. And this power still remains with them, except so far as they have

Exhibit 2.1 The Attorney General's response to the Aldephi decision.

"Garden City, L.I., March 24 – Attorney General Dennis C. Vacco sued Adelphi University's former trustees today to recover millions of dollars he said they had misspent on a lavish life style for the college's president.

'We hold the board members personally liable for any misspent money', Mr. Vacco said at a news conference at State Supreme court here, a few minutes drive from the Adelphi campus.

The suit also seeks restitution of $3.1 million in legal fees spent to defend the former Adelphi officials who were ousted last month by the State Board of Regents. In addition, it accuses the trustees of breaching their responsibilities by allowing two trustees to do business with Adelphi.

The suit did not specify the grand total sought. 'We're talking, ballpark, several million dollars', Mr. Vacco said. Any funds recovered would be returned to Adelphi, he added.

The suit seeks recovery of funds from those who benefited from the improper payments as well as those who approved or allowed them.

Source: Lambert, 1997.

delegated a portion of it to the federal government. The sovereign will is made known to us by legislative enactment. The state, as a sovereign, is the parens patriae" [*Mormon Church* v. *United States*, 1890].

Many attorneys general have relatively broad powers to review the activities of charities to ensure they are acting in the public interest. For example, in New York, "the attorney general may institute appropriate proceedings to secure compliance with this section and to secure the proper administration of any trust, corporation or other relationship to which this section applies. The powers and duties of the attorney general provided in this section are in addition to his existing powers and duties. No court shall modify or terminate the powers and responsibilities of any trust, corporation or other relationship unless the attorney general is a party to the proceeding." The statute makes clear that its terms apply to "any non-profit corporation organized under the laws of this state for charitable purposes" (New York State Consolidated Laws, Chapter 17B, Article 8, Part 1.4).

The attorney general of Pennsylvania puts it this way in the *Handbook for Charitable Nonprofit Organizations:* "The Attorney General, as parens patriae of charities, has a duty to protect the public's interest in the charitable assets held by nonprofit corporations." This power is rarely exercised: "Criminal prosecutions of NPO's are rare. Of about 200,000 serious federal prosecutions in 1984–7, only 1,569 were organizations, and of 1,221 of those convicted less than 1 percent were other-than-profit business organizations. About half of all corporate prosecutions also involve officers and employees" (Oleck, 1992, p. 137).

A striking example is a 1996 case from Virginia: a dispute about the control of a nonprofit organization. On one side was a group of independent directors and on the other a group of directors affiliated with an ex-felon who was attempting to reassert control. The Virginia attorney general was asked to use his plenary powers to intervene in the case but failed to do so, and the state supreme court determined that the failure to follow the election procedures as provided in the by-laws invalidated the election of the independent directors despite the fact that they had already served for four years. As a result of this decision, the felon who had been convicted of racketeering and taking kickbacks while a member of a school board and his affiliates were left in control of the charity (*Stewart et al.* v. *Lady et al.*, 1996).

Perhaps in an effort to fulfill their "parens patriae" duty to protect the public's interest in charities, the attorneys general of sixteen states and the District of Columbia recently issued a report expressing concerns about relationships between nonprofit organizations and commercial entities. The attorneys general expressed concern

> that commercial-nonprofit product advertisements often communicate the false and misleading messages that the products have been endorsed by the nonprofit partner in the commercial-nonprofit relationship and that such products are superior to other competing products. The Attorneys General are concerned that some promotions may further mislead the public about the effect consumers' purchases may have on the level of

charitable contributions the commercial sponsor will make. Additionally, such joint advertising campaigns using a respected nonprofit's name and logo often fail to provide important information consumers need in order to make informed choices, including the facts that the commercial sponsor has paid the nonprofit organization for use of its name and logo and, as is often the case, that the relationship between the corporate sponsor and the nonprofit is exclusive in nature [Attorney General of New York, 1999].

Given that the attorney general of any state can prosecute fraud or the making of false and misleading statements in either commercial or nonprofit messages, this report takes on additional significance and should be a warning to nonprofit managers about the possible consequences of such violations.

Finally, although the focus here has been on the role of the board or other managers of charities and the organization's potential liability, it is more than a mere corollary that there is individual culpability for violation of the law. Individuals can be held responsible simply for not behaving as what the law defines as a "reasonable, prudent person." This is the same standard, for example, as is used in commercial cases where fiduciaries such as a Board of Directors are expected to exercise reasonable "business judgment." New York State again provides one example of the standard of care to which directors and officers of a nonprofit corporation must subscribe. Not-For-Profit Corporation Law § 171(a), requires that the directors must "discharge the duties of their respective positions in good faith and with that degree of diligence, care and skill which ordinarily prudent men would exercise under similar circumstances in like positions." As fiduciaries, board members owe a duty to the corporation and "may not profit improperly at the expense of their corporation" (*Turner* v. *American Metal Co.*, 268 App Div. 239, 273, *appeal dismissed* 295 NY 822; see also *Gedded v. Anaconda Min. Co.*, 254 US 590, 599).

In the Adelphi case already referred to (see Exhibit 2.1), the board of regents said:

Finally, we find that the trustees cannot rely on the "business judgment rule" to protect them from removal on this record. . . . The rule does not shield from scrutiny irrational decisions that are based on inadequate information or consideration. It is simply no defense where, as here, trustees have wholly failed to exercise any judgment whatsoever. Nor can the trustees invoke the rule's protections when they have failed to exercise the degree of care and diligence which ordinary persons in their positions would exercise. When directors act blindly, recklessly and heedlessly, as these trustees have in setting [President] Diamandopoulos' compensation, they cannot escape responsibility for their conduct" (Antally, 1998).

Punitive damages can be also awarded against nonprofit organizations and presumably also against their directors. For example, a California court awarded punitive damages from the Church of Scientology for infliction of mental suffering (*Wollersheim* v. *Church of Scientology*, 1989).

Individuals associated with nonprofit organizations may also be prosecuted for direct violation of criminal statutes, as William Aramony, former president of United Way of America, found that out with his sentencing for multiple crimes in 1995. After a jury trial, Aramony and codefendants were convicted of numerous violations of federal laws for participating in a scheme to defraud the United Way of America. Aramony was convicted of conspiracy to defraud the United States by impeding the lawful functions of the IRS, six counts of mail fraud, two counts of wire fraud, nine counts of engaging in the interstate transportation of fraudulently acquired property, two counts of engaging in monetary transactions in the proceeds of specified unlawful activity, three counts of filing false tax returns, and two counts of aiding the filing of false tax returns. And Daniel Wiant of the Ohio chapter of the American Cancer Society was sentenced in 2001 as a first offender to "thirteen years after pleading guilty to stealing eight million dollars of charity funds" (BBC.CO.UK, 2001).

Conclusion

The ultimate control over charities rests with neither the board nor the government but rather with donors who can withhold resources from charities that do not behave as they wish. The board may well be the next best opportunity to ensure accountability and to be certain the nonprofit organization is true to its goals and its responsibilities.

All else failing, the state may intervene. Sometimes governments intervene because someone in authority does not like decisions made properly or in good faith. Sometimes the intervention may be best explained by political motivation.

Enforcement, Politics and Accountability

As is true of all government regulation whether by civil or criminal laws, the decision of whether and when to intervene is made by politically elected or appointed officials. Thus, such decisions can, on occasion, be politically motivated and there can be differing views of whether enforcement activities are truly "in the public interest."

For example, in one case the IRS had held a fundraiser to be an "insider" due to the degree of control of the fundraiser over the charity. The effect of being held to be an insider was the retroactive revocation of exempt status. The appellate court reversed saying there was no evidence that the fundraiser was other than a contracted agent of the charity simply because the results of the fundraising was a very high cost of fundraising. The court held that the fact that the fundraiser made a lot of money did not constitute private inurement. (*United Cancer Council* v. *Com'nr.*, 7th Cir. 1999). See http://www.laws.findlaw.com/7th/982181.html.

In another recent case, the Illinois Attorney General sued claiming fraud and breach of fiduciary duty because a telemarketer retained 85% of the funds donated to a charity. "The complaint further alleged that defendants, by failing to reveal to donors the percentage of the contribution which would actually go to the charity, obtained money from donors under false pretenses." The Illinois Supreme Court affirmed the dismissal of the complaint under the longstanding principles of decisions by the Supreme Court of the United States that the cost of fundraising percentage or ratio is not a valid basis upon which to allege fraud and that such efforts impinge upon the 1st Amendment free speech rights of nonprofits (*Illinois* v. *Telemarketing Associations*, 2001).

Nevertheless, whether governmental authority is exercised properly or not, it is clear that when accountability fails at other levels, there is at a minimum, the authority for the government to intervene under certain circumstances even such intervention rarely occurs.

References

Atnally, E."Guidance for Those Serving on the Boards of Not-for-Profit Organizations." *New York State Bar Journal*, Vol. 70, No. 6, September–October 1998. Available at http://www.nysba.org/media/barjournal/atnally.html

Attorney General of New York, *What's in a Nonprofit's Name?* Albany, NY: Office of the New York State Attorney General Eliot Spitzer, April 6, 1999. Available at http://www.oag.state.ny.us/press/reports/nonprofit/full_text.html

Attorney General of Pennsylvania. *Handbook for Charitable Nonprofit Organizations.* Harrisburg, PA: Office of the Attorney General of Pennsylvania, undated. Available at http://www.attorneygeneral.gov/pei/brochures/charities/html/handbook.cfm

BBC.CO.UK. "Charity employee sentenced in $8m fraud." 2001. Available at http://news.bbc.co.uk/hi/english/world/americas/newsid_1275000/1275119.stm

Better Business Bureau. Philanthropic Advisory Service. May 2001. Available at http://www.bbb.org/about/pas.asp

Bograd, H. "Alerting Nonprofit Boards to Financial Trouble." Unpublished paper, Oct. 28, 1995. Available at http://www.charitychannel.com/GuestShare/Harriet_Bograd/

Copilevitz, E., and Raney, W. "Overlapping Layers of Charitable Solicitation and Fundraising Regulation." In R. Fuerst (ed.), *What Fundraisers Need to Know About State and Federal Regulation*, 1996.

Covington, S. "Who Governs the Non-Profit Sector?" *Fund Raising Management*, 1994, *33*, 25.

Evangelical Council for Financial Accountability.*Top Ten ECFA Field Review Issues.* Winchester, VA: Evangelical Council for Financial Accountability, August 2000.

Evangelical Council for Financial Accountability, *Commentary on ECFA Standard #2.* Winchester, VA: Evangelical Council for Financial Accountability, n.d. [2000]. See also http://www.ecfamembers.org

Lambert, B. "State Sues to Recover Funds Spent by Adelphi's Ex-Trustees." *The New York Times*, March 25, 1997, p. B5.

McGovern, J. "Exempt Organizations Update: What's Hot in Washington." Washington, D.C.: KPMG, Inc., February 2000. See http://www.independentsector.org/programs/gr/Feb_2000_newsletter.html

Mayer, L. "Proposed Intermediate Sanctions Regulations." Washington, DC: Caplin & Drysdale, September 1998. Available at http://www.charitychannel.com/guestshare/caplindrysdale/. at VI. A. 2.

Mormon Church v. United States, 136 U.S. 1, 57 (1890).
Oleck, H. *Nonprofit Corporations, Organizations and Associations.* (5th ed.) Englewood Cliffs, N.J.: Prentice Hall, 1992.
Parker, J. S. "Criminal Sentencing Policy for Organizations." *American Criminal Law Review*, 1989, *26*, 513–604.
Smith, E. B. "Comment." *University of San Francisco Law Review*, 1990, *24*, 653–675.
Stewart et al. v. Lady et al. Supreme Court of Virginia, No. 950850, 251 Va. 106, 465 S.E. 2d 782. January 12, 1996.
U.S. Postal Service. *Nonprofit Standard Mail Eligibility: Nonprofit and Other Qualified Organizations.* (Publication #417). Washington, D.C.: U.S. Postal Service, October, 1996, 19–22.
Wright, C. D. "Revised Conflicts of Interest Policy Is Mere Refinement, Owens Says." *Exempt Organizations Tax Review*, 1997, *18*, 194.

GEOFFREY PETERS *is president of Creative Direct Marketing International and pro-bono counsel of American Charities for Reasonable Fundraising Regulation.*

The perfect evaluation system that will clearly and objectively reveal how well your nonprofit organization is performing may never be found. But here is a review of three approaches to evaluation that show promise.

3

The state of evaluation tools and systems for nonprofit organizations

Vic Murray

MANY NONPROFIT organizations are feeling pressure from funders, government contractors, and clients to show that they are "making a difference." They eagerly seek valid and reliable measurements that will yield clear indicators of how well they are doing. Many also yearn for proven best practices for managing their organizations, which, when implemented, will ensure that they run efficiently and effectively. If they are unable to show directly the impact of their efforts, at least they can assure concerned stakeholders that they are doing things the way they ought to be done.

Is there a set of performance indicators that many different kinds of charitable organizations can easily apply and will yield the clear picture of impact that stakeholders want? Are there universally agreed-on best practices applicable to all nonprofits that have been proven to increase performance? This chapter looks at the answers to these questions by reviewing a few of the systems put forward as usable for assessing performance in the nonprofit sector. In a nutshell, this appraisal concludes that the answer to both of these questions is, "Not yet." Nevertheless, there are some promising leads in the form of processes that a nonprofit organization and its stakeholders can adopt that could help improve the analysis of performance and lead to better decisions on needed changes that are right for it (if not for others).

Characteristics of good evaluation systems

In order to evaluate the evaluation systems, we need first to have a clear idea about what an ideal evaluation system would look like. In a nutshell, it would need to meet several criteria:

- A clear statement of that which is to be evaluated. Standard evaluation texts (Mark, Henry, and Julnes, 2000; Sonnichsen, 2000) point out that many things can be evaluated. For example, one can evaluate the performance of individuals in specific jobs or focus instead on the evaluation of programs or functions within an organization. Sometimes the interest is in the whole organization or even larger systems of which organizations are a part (an example is the child welfare system). The distinction among these focal points for evaluations can be called the level at which it occurs.

Evaluation systems also differ in terms of what they measure within a level. The distinction is typically made between measuring inputs, processes, or outputs and outcomes. Input measures count what goes into a program or organization, such as dollars invested, human resources, or equipment. Process and output measures count activities undertaken and services or products produced, such as the amount of staff training carried out or the number of clients served. Outcomes measure the results of the activities and the extent to which they achieved the objectives for which they were designed.

- A statement of the objectives of that which is being evaluated. In order to determine how well a person, program, or organization is doing, the objectives they are working toward should be SMART—the acronym for specific, measurable, achievable, relevant, and timebound, that is, explicit in terms of the time in which they are to be achieved.

- A clear statement of the standards to be applied in interpreting the indicators used. These standards should reveal whether that which was evaluated performed above or below expectations.
- An understanding of what evaluation results mean. Can one make an inference about the performance of an organization from an evaluation of its programs or infer the outcomes of an action from a measurement of its outputs? These kinds of inferences are what professional evaluators call logic models. There are two basic logic models required. Measurement logic models make clear the assumed links between input indicators and process indicators, process indicators and outcome indicators, and outcome indicators and goals. They should also identify the other factors that affect the indicators at each stage but are not directly controllable by those responsible. Level of focus logic models link evaluations between levels. That is, they make explicit the links between evaluations of individuals, programs or functions, organizations, and larger systems.
- An evaluation system that is implemented consistently over time and with integrity by all those involved.

The only problem with this ideal approach to evaluation is that it is virtually impossible to reach if we are talking about evaluating human behavior in real life (not laboratory) situations, and this difficulty most emphatically applies to organizations in the nonprofit sector. Measuring inputs and counting outputs may be relatively easy, but the big problem is interpreting what they mean. The temptation is great to infer that more inputs and more outputs means that outcomes are being achieved better. Similarly, it is tempting to infer that if individuals or specific programs perform well, the whole organization and even the system of which it is a part will also be performing well. Properly developed logic models attempt to make explicit the inferred causal connections between levels and types of measurement and demonstrate their validity. But most evaluation systems do not require thinking these logic models through before they are implemented.

Similarly, even if the logic models are fully spelled out, it is difficult to make program or organizational objectives SMART. How exactly does one make specific and measurable an art gallery's mission "to enrich and enliven the human spirit through art"? The time dimension is also difficult to track. The Scout movement aims to produce better citizens, but the proof of their success may not be evident for many years after children were exposed to the program.

In much of the nonprofit world, it is still far too early to proclaim standards and benchmarks for measuring performance between nonprofit organizations in the same field of endeavor or even between programs within the same organization. In addition, most nonprofits have far too little time, money, or in-house skills for developing evaluation systems and maintaining them over time. These limitations make achieving the desired levels of validity and reliability very difficult.

Because of all these inherent difficulties and the inescapable elements of subjectivity in evaluation systems, they are subject to many common human foibles. If any of the parties involved in the process sense that it might not be fair, or believe that its results might be interpreted using political, personal, or ideological criteria different from their own, or think the results will make them look incompetent, they will be tempted to subvert the process. This is called the "look good, avoid blame" phenomenon (Cutt and Murray, 2000, p. 39), and it can result in negative information being covered up and other information being distorted or given a slanted interpretation.

Existing evaluation tools and approaches

Given these problems with evaluation systems in general, what can one say about the pros and cons of some existing evaluation tools and approaches? We look at three tools that show promise for evaluating an organization as a whole. These systems have not themselves been evaluated. There is no widely disseminated information on how widely they have been adopted, how long they have remained in place once adopted, or how satisfied the users of the systems are.[1] All are intended primarily for use within the organization by its board or management team as a way of assessing organizational performance.

Program Outcomes: The United Way Approach

This evaluation system (http://www.unitedway.org/outcomes) focuses exclusively on identifying and measuring program outcomes for agencies funded by the United Way. Although the system starts by evaluating results at the program level, these are supposed to be aggregated at the organizational level by member agencies to report on their effectiveness.

The outcome information is intended to be used by the United Way to help member agencies improve program performance, identify and achieve United Way priorities (funding allocation criteria), and broaden the base of financial and volunteer support (fundraising). Implementation of the outcome measurement system occurs in six stages:

1. Building agency commitment and clarifying expectations
2. Building agency capacity to measure outcomes
3. Identifying outcomes, indicators, and data collection methods
4. Collecting and analyzing outcome data
5. Improving the outcome measurement system
6. Using and communicating outcome information

The United Way has developed a set of guiding principles and specific steps to help member agencies complete each stage of the implementation process. Rather than advocate one particular way to develop outcomes or collect outcome data, the United Way uses a checklist approach to encourage agencies to think more broadly and critically about the measurement process. For example, agencies are asked about the validity, reliability, sensitivity to client characteristics, and ability to capture longer-term results of their proposed data collection methods but are not told which ones to use.

The outcome measurement system does not specify the type of evaluation standards to be used but does suggest that target-based absolute standards and time-based relative standards are best.

Agencies are not expected to establish targets until they have at least one year of baseline data. The system discourages the use of benchmark-based relative standards or those that involve comparison with similar programs that are considered exemplary until accurate outcome data are available. It is generally understood that in the first few years of an outcome measurement system, the data often say more about what is wrong with the evaluation system than what is taking place in the programs.

Recent research reported on the United Way Web site suggests general satisfaction with the six-stage process it recommends and the proper way to develop the outcome measurement system. This process is the most sensitive to the importance of implementation of the three reviewed here. It is strongly recommended as a model to consider but would be best used in conjunction with either or both of the other two systems, which are more process oriented.

The Balanced Scorecard

This multiattribute system for conceptualizing and measuring performance (http://www.balancedscorecard.org) was designed originally for business organizations and currently is being adapted for nonprofit organizations. In its original form, it assumes that the primary goal of a business is long-run profit maximization. It argues that this will be achieved through a "balanced scorecard of performance attributes" grouped around four perspectives:

- The financial perspective, which measures various financial performance indicators of primary interest to shareholders
- The customer perspective, comprising measures of customer satisfaction
- The internal business perspective, which measures internal efficiency and quality
- The innovation and learning perspective, which attempts to measure the organization's ability to adapt to changes required by a changing environment

In the case of nonprofit organizations, their mission statement becomes the end point to be reached through these perspectives.

The process starts with defining what that is and identifying outcome indicators that will reveal the extent to which it is being achieved. For nonprofits, *customers* must be replaced by *clients* or *users* of the organization's services, and the financial perspective becomes that of the funders or potential funders. This adaptation is illustrated in Figure 3.1. Although there is still a great deal of work to do to flesh out exactly how to apply this system to nonprofit organizations, it shows considerable promise.

Canadian Comprehensive Auditing Foundation Framework for Performance Reporting

This is the most significant Canadian effort at tackling the value-for-money issue in both the public and the nonprofit sectors (http://www.ccaf-fcvi.com). The Canadian Comprehensive Auditing Foundation (CCAF) Framework for Performance Reporting puts forward twelve attributes of effectiveness suggesting that organizations can be audited in terms of how well they manifest these attributes. In this sense, it can be focused at either the organization or the program and function levels and is intended to help evaluators get a clear picture of how effectively and efficiently the mission is being

Figure 3.1. Balanced scorecard model for nonprofit organizations

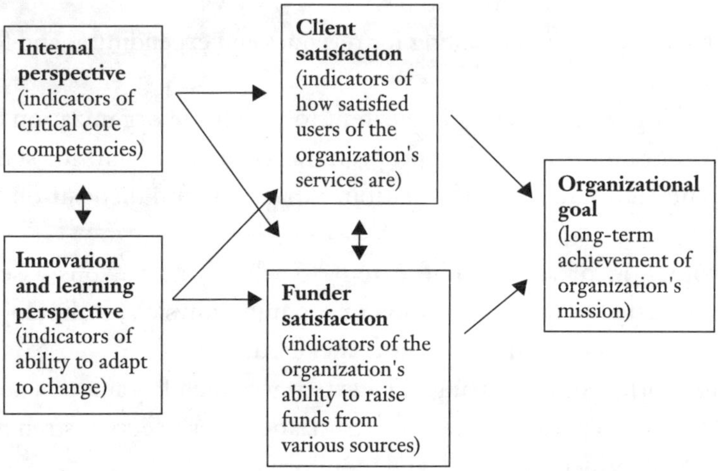

achieved. It is similar in many ways to the Balanced Scorecard, although the details of implementation are more thorough.

The system involves developing indicators for the following twelve attributes of effectiveness:

Management direction: The extent to which programmatic objectives are clearly stated and understood

Relevance: The extent to which the organization or program continues to make sense with respect to the problems or conditions to which it was intended to respond

Appropriateness: The extent to which the design of the organization or program and the level of effort are logical in relation to their objectives

Achievement of intended results: The extent to which the goals and objectives have been achieved

Acceptance: The extent to which the stakeholders for whom the organization or program is designed judge it to be satisfactory

Secondary impacts: The extent to which significant consequences, either intended or unintended and either positive or negative, have occurred

Costs and productivity: The relationship between costs, inputs, and outputs

Responsiveness: The capacity of the program or organization to adapt to changes in such factors as markets, competition, available funding, and technology

Financial results: Accounting for revenues and expenditures and for assets and liabilities

Working environment: The extent to which the organization or program provides an appropriate work environment for staff, and staff have the information, capacities, and disposition to serve the objectives

Protection of assets: The extent to which the various assets entrusted to the organization or program (physical, technological, financial, and human) are safeguarded

Monitoring and reporting: The extent to which key matters pertaining to performance and organizational or program strength are identified, reported, and monitored

The system thus encompasses both process and outcome elements, although the former are dominant. Although there is no publicly available information on how effective this evaluation system is, there is potential in trying to merge it with the Balanced Scorecard approach. At present the Balanced Scorecard is short on the specifics that should come under each of its four perspectives, especially with regard to nonprofit organizations. The CCAF approach offers more detail but lacks the conceptual framework that shows how their 12 attributes relate to one another. This is provided by the Balanced Scorecard. Figure 3.2 illustrates how the two approaches might fit together.

Charities Rating Services

There are also several evaluation systems developed to help funders and the public decide how effective various charities are.[2] All of these systems try to offer generic standards that will reveal how well a nonprofit organization is managed. The problem is that in trying to compare organizations with so many different missions, the standards make no reference to outcomes and do not attempt to reveal the measurement or level logic models they are built on. Instead, they assume that organizations that meet their process standards will be more likely to be effective in achieving their goals. Regrettably,

Figure 3.2. Illustration of how the Balanced Scorecard and CCAF frameworks could be strengthened through integration

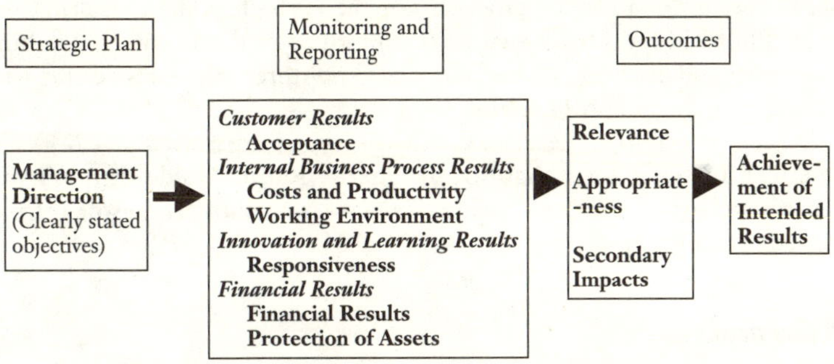

Note: CCAF attributes are presented in bold type. Balanced Scorecard attributes are presented in bold italics.

there is little or no published research that supports these assumptions, although it may be that those who most severely violate the standards they measure are less likely to be effective. Whether those that best meet or surpass these standards are comparatively more effective, however, is unknown.

Another problem with all of the evaluation tools except the United Way approach is that little attention is paid to how the evaluation system is to be implemented. A great deal of research has concluded that unless all those to be affected by an evaluation system have a strong voice in its design and accept the final product, there is a high probability that the system will fail (Cutt and Murray, 2000; Mark, Henry, and Julnes, 2000; Sonnichsen, 2000).

Conclusion

It appears that there is still a long way to go before there will be available a tried and tested evaluation system that can be applied by most nonprofit organizations to reveal a valid picture of how well they are performing. Some would argue there is no point in trying, yet decisions are made every day based on untested assumptions and idiosyncratic perceptions of performance. The goal of trying to move the dialogue on this process to a more rational, data-based approach is worth pursuing.

Notes

1. For an excellent source of information on the pros and cons of a wide range of evaluation tools and processes, see the Web site of the Canadian Centre for Philanthropy: http://www.ccp.ca/information/documents/gd44h.htm. It identifies and provides commentary on twenty-three Web sites dealing with evaluation in the nonprofit sector.

2. See, for example, the Wise Giving Alliance (http://www.give.org), the American Institute for Philanthropy Charity Rating Guide (http://www.charitywatch.org), and the Charities Review Council of Minnesota (http://www.crcmn.org).

References

Cutt, J., and Murray, V. *Accountability and Effectiveness Evaluation in Non-Profit Organizations.* New York: Routledge, 2000.

Mark, M. M., Henry, G. T., and Julnes, G. *Evaluation: An Integrated Framework for Understanding, Guiding, and Improving Policies and Programs.* San Francisco: Jossey-Bass, 2000.

Sonnichsen, R. C. *High Impact Internal Evaluation.* Thousand Oaks, Calif.: Sage, 2000.

VIC MURRAY *is an adjunct professor in the School of Public Administration, University of Victoria, Victoria, British Columbia, Canada.*

Internal and external forms of nonprofit self-regulation are explored using evaluation results from Minnesota, a state associated with innovation in nonprofit accountability initiatives.

4

Accountability, organizational capacity, and continuous improvement: Findings from Minnesota's nonprofit sector

Angela L. Bies

MINNESOTA'S NONPROFIT sector provides an important context for examining accountability reforms and related organizational responses. Minnesota has historically enjoyed a rich tradition of individual and institutional philanthropy, a vigorous nonprofit economy, an active state charity regulation function, and strong statewide nonprofit advocacy and training organizations (Minnesota Council of Nonprofits, 1998). Minnesota also provides insight into an early accountability reform model evidenced in the work of a statewide nonprofit industry self-regulation, or

Note: An earlier version of this chapter was presented at the Annual Meeting of the Association for Research on Nonprofit Organizations and Voluntary Action in New Orleans, November 16, 2000. The author was Executive Director of the Charities Review Council prior to conducting this research. Frances Lawrenz, T. Marshall Egan, Anne Fluekiger and Gabrielle Schmiegel served as external reviewers and staff and board members of the Charities Review Council assisted with the conduct of the evaluation study described here.

watchdog, agency, the Charities Review Council, founded in 1946. More recent innovations include the 1998 establishment of a voluntary set of Principles and Practices for Nonprofit Excellence by the statewide nonprofit association, the Minnesota Council of Nonprofits (MCN). In addition, several key statewide and local institutional funders have engaged in outcomes-based evaluation requirements. Several prominent Minnesota-based nonprofit organizations have also been active in the Total Quality Management movement or have adopted voluntary professional codes of ethics like those of the Association of Fundraising Professionals (until recently known as the National Society of Fund Raising Executives [NSFRE]).

An examination of Minnesota's nonprofit accountability landscape is useful both for its importance as a relatively successful and active nonprofit economy and because of its tradition as an early adopter of external and internal nonprofit accountability innovations. Minnesota's nonprofit sector also provides a critical case in terms of its adoption of certain continuous improvement or organizational learning practices, development of internal organizational capacities, and responses to external accountability demands. This chapter outlines findings from a comprehensive evaluation study commissioned by the statewide watchdog agency and provides insight into organizational responses to accountability mandates.

Defining accountability

Because the term *accountability* is associated with various, often abstract, and sometimes competing conceptualizations in the literature, specific definitions are necessary to clarify meaning and establish boundaries for the use of this term. Accountability is generally defined as the means by which individuals and organizations are answerable to others and are held responsible by their actions (Schene, 1991; Edwards and Hulme, 1996a, 1996b; Kearns, 1996). Mandatory and discretionary self-regulation models are well-known approaches to nonprofit accountability throughout the world. These competing models pose alternative policy and practice considerations. Mandatory self-regulation models are characterized by the existence of external actors, such as funders or outside regulators, who monitor nonprofit accountability and either reward or sanction nonprofits based on their level of implementation of accountability practices. Discretionary self-regulation models are characterized by internal organizational mechanisms, such as learning and skilled and responsible administration, being associated with the adoption and implementation of accountability practices.

Kearns (1996) identifies two fundamental questions embedded in these basic definitions of accountability: To whom are nonprofits accountable? and For what are these organizations responsible? This chapter addresses these questions by exploring theoretical frameworks useful to understanding mandatory and discretionary forms of self-regulation, historical roots and contemporary trends influencing accountability, briefly reviewing the literature on nonprofit accountability, and examining prevalent approaches to accountability underway in Minnesota's nonprofit sector.

Theoretical frameworks: Institutional and learning theories

Theories that relate to organizational action, structure or form, and environments, such as institutional and resource-dependence theory, provide prominent frameworks for studying nonprofit responses to externally driven accountability. Over the past two decades, theories of organizational action have included resource dependence (Pfeffer and Salancik, 1978), population ecology (Hannan and Freeman, 1977, 1984), contingency theory (Child, 1972; Miller and Friesen, 1984; Mintzberg, 1979, 1981), transaction cost economics (Williamson, 1975, 1981, 1985), and institutional theory (DiMaggio and Powell, 1983; Meyer and Rowan, 1977; Scott, 1995; Zucker, 1983, 1987). Such theories assist understanding of mandatory self-regulation, in which organizational responses to accountability are associated with externally driven consequences in the form of sanctions or rewards. Theories related to organizational learning or continuous improvement (OL/CI) provide insight into the processes of discretionary self-regulation, in which internal organizational processes and capacity are associated with the implementation of accountability practices.

In the private, public, and nonprofit sectors, learning is often tied to the effectiveness of organizations. In the nonprofit context, such learning is vital because of the increasingly central role that nonprofits play. In addition to recognizing the vital roles of nonprofits, increased attention is being paid to the training and learning needs of nongovernmental organizations (NGOs) (Edwards, 1997; Fowler, 1997). Both practitioner and academic literature in the field of management are rich with examples in which learning theories are coupled with organizational performance (Drucker, 1964; Handy, 1993; Letts et al., 1999; Swanson and Houlton, 1999; Gilley and Maycunich, 2000). Similar couplings are presented in the small but growing body of literature related to OL/CI and the operations of nonprofit organizations (Edwards, 1997; Edwards and Hulme, 1992, 1996a). In their work related primarily to international nongovernmental organizations, Edwards and Hulme (1996b) extend this discussion by linking organizational learning to the following areas of nonprofit operations: identification of cost-effective practices; understanding the impact of wider forces (such as social and economic considerations) on nonprofits and vice versa; as a foundation for accountability and dissemination of results information; understanding changes in the external environment, including changes in donor policies; staff development; continuous improvement; and knowledge transfer to other nonprofits.

Although in the past, nonprofits may have been somewhat protected from demands for learning due to a history of loyal or well-aligned relationships with donors, changes in funding and social environments mandate responsive, accountable nonprofits that are equipped to solve complex social problems (Edwards and Hulme, 1996a). The concepts of OL/CI provide an alternative theoretical perspective to inform the study of nonprofit accountability. The process of implementing accountability practices involves organizational change, internal motivation and mechanisms, and learning. This is especially true in the discretionary self-regulation model, which involves self-direction to adopt and implement accountability practices.

Organizational learning is conceptualized in a variety of ways. One prominent conceptualization is that organizational learning occurs when "individuals within an organization experience a problematic situation and inquire into it on the organization's behalf . . . and respond to that mismatch through a process of thought and further action" (Argyris and Schön, 1996, p. 16). Similar to organizational learning, continuous improvement has been defined variously as it has developed from a theoretical concept to a practical concept. Detert, Kopel, Mauriel, and Jenni (2000) encompass elements of the earlier work of Deming (1986), Juran (1988), and Argyris and Schön (1974) and view CI as a set of practices and philosophies embodied in the following categories: a long-term orientation and openness to change, customer input and customer focus, data-based decision-making, studying and evaluating processes, leadership, systems thinking, and training. Argyris and Schön (1974, 1996) further distinguish between *espoused* theories, the explanations used to describe or predict behavior, and *theories-in-use*, which account for actual behaviors in organizations. In the realm of nonprofit accountability, this might be illustrated by contrasting an organization's stated accountability values with its demonstration of practices.

Although the study reported on in this chapter centers on an evaluation of nonprofits that are engaged in a mandatory form of self-regulation, it sought also to provide a preliminary exploration of the proposed relationship between OL/CI and the demonstration of certain nonprofit accountability practices. Such OL/CI elements include involving key leaders with accountability policy and practices, integrating accountability into strategic or long-range planning, employing internally driven forms of self-regulation, such as adherence to voluntary standards or codes of ethics, and integrating learning from accountability reviews or evaluation into organizational practices. A shortcoming of organizational learning theory, however, is the limited empirical evidence related to its effectiveness. Although prevalent in academic and practitioner literature, organizational learning operates as more of a management concept than an empirically supported theory. As such, it is insufficient to describe fully the processes of organizational learning associated with the implementation of mandatory or discretionary forms of nonprofit self-regulation. For these reasons, this chapter suggests future research necessary to explore the proposed relationship between CI/OL and nonprofit accountability initiatives.

Accountability: Landscape and literature

Because nonprofit organizations are often characterized by their unique role of existing to serve the public good, nonprofit actors are often called on to respond to criteria or standards beyond individual pursuits, provincial or idiosyncratic interests, or personal gain. Such criteria or standards define the roles and expectations of various nonprofit stakeholders, including individual and institutional donors, nonprofits themselves, and communities served by nonprofits. Although the literature related to accountability in the private and public sectors is rich (Schene, 1991; Kearns, 1996), far less has been written about nonprofit accountability. A review of the limited literature of historic and contemporary nonprofit accountability uncovers examples of persistent and increasing calls for accountability.

In the U.S. nonprofit context, the history of mandatory self-regulation models begins in 1918 with the creation of the National Charities Information Bureau (NCIB).[1] With a mission of "promoting informed giving," NCIB was founded by "a group of national citizen leaders concerned that Americans were giving millions of dollars to charitable organizations, particularly war relief organizations, that they knew little or nothing about" (NCIB, 1996, p. 1). In a similar spirit, the Charities Review Council, when formed in Minneapolis in 1946, was designed in response to the rapid growth of the charitable sector in Minnesota's booming post–World War II economy (Pratt, 1999).

Since 1960, numerous review agencies have been established within the nonprofit sector and its subsectors. The following limited list illustrates the wide range of focus of such initiatives: InterAction, operating in the realm of foreign assistance organizations; American Institute of Philanthropy; Philanthropic Advisory Service (PAS) of the Better Business Bureau; and Evangelical Council for Financial Accountability, operating in the realm of Christian relief organizations (Bothwell, 1999). The establishment of monitoring entities has been accompanied by the development of discretionary self-regulation models such as codes of ethics or voluntary standards designed to promote accountable behavior by nonprofits and people working in nonprofit contexts. Examples of such codes of ethics include standards of ethical practice by NSFRE (now AFP), voluntary standards established by several statewide nonprofit associations including initiatives in Maryland and Minnesota, and Principles for Effective Grantmakers by the Council on Foundations (INDEPENDENT SECTOR, 2000). Similarly, numerous organizations and services have been established to provide financial and programmatic information about nonprofits to the public. GuideStar, a searchable Web-based database, is one such service. (See Table 4.1.) The increasing number of these and similar initiatives, particularly over the past two decades, indicates that interest in and activity related to nonprofit accountability are issues of ongoing relevance (Bothwell, 1999; Edwards and Hulme, 1996b). Prior to analyzing the appropriateness or efficacy of various accountability-focused activities, it is important to consider the motivating forces and underlying assumptions driving such initiatives.

The following factors are associated with intensified interest in nonprofit accountability:

insufficient government oversight

absence of direct voter or stakeholder regulation as exists in government and the private sectors

rapid growth in U.S. individual and institutional philanthropy

increasing number of nonprofits; increasing size, assets, and influence of nonprofits

Table 4.1. Nonprofit accountability resources

Organization	*Accountability Guidelines*	*Web Site References*
American Institute of Philanthropy	Assesses charities using criteria it has developed for analyzing financial and operating data	http://www.charitywatch.org/criteria.html
Association of Fundraising Professionals	Code of Ethical Principles and Standards of Professional Practice	http://www.nsfre.org/ethics/code_and_standards
BBB Wise Giving Alliance (Better Business Bureau)	Council of Better Business Bureau's Standards for Charitable Solicitations	http://www.give.org/standards/cbbbstds.asp
Charities Review Council	Accountability Standards	http://www.crcmn.org/standards/index.htm
	CBBB Standards for Charitable Solicitations	http://www.bbb.org/about/charstandard.asp
Evangelical Council for Financial Accountability	Seven Standards of Responsible Stewardship	http://www.ecfa.org/7standards.asp
Guidestar	A database of nonprofit organizations, based on self-reports and IRS Form 990 reports	http://www.guidestar.org/
InterAction	Private Voluntary Organization Standards	http://www.interaction.org/pvostandards/index.html
Maryland Nonprofits	Standards for Excellence	http://www.mdnonprofit.org/sfex_intro.htm
Minnesota Council of Nonprofits	Principles and Practices for Nonprofit Excellence	http://www.mncn.org/pnp_index.htm

increasing reliance on nonprofits for delivery of necessary aspects of civil society and social programs

increasing media coverage and public scrutiny resulting from scandals in the nonprofit sector

shift from government funding toward direct funding of nonprofits

a belief that increased accountability fosters public trust in the nonprofit sector

a belief that increased accountability will result in greater nonprofit efficiency and effectiveness a belief that self-regulation will prevent unnecessary or burdensome government oversight

and a belief that accountability is inherently "the right thing to do" (Edwards and Hulme, 1996a, 1996b; Bell and Brown, 1997; Eisenberg, 1997; Bothwell, 1999; INDEPENDENT SECTOR, 2000; Light, 2000).

Despite a proliferation of nonprofit accountability initiatives worldwide, scant evidence stemming from rigorous research on nonprofit accountability exists (Hall, 1987; Kearns, 1994; Edwards and Hulme, 1996a, 1996b; Eisenberg, 1997). Although the conceptual and descriptive literature related to private and public sector accountability is substantial from both historical and current perspectives (Estes, Biney, and Bergthold, 1989; Kearns, 1994; Schene, 1991), literature on nonprofit accountability is far less extensive. Studies that do exist focus on nonprofit accountability in a general sense, outlining dimensions of accountability and various definitions and conceptualizations. Several studies provide an overview of nonprofit accountability from historical and disciplinary perspectives and include Lawry's study linking accountability to managerial ethics (1995), Hammack's historical perspective (1995), and Chisolm's legal perspective (1995).

The literature specifically addressing accountability in nonprofits includes numerous pieces related to financial accountability, as well as descriptive or practical treatment of accountability (Schene, 1991; Kearns, 1996; Bothwell, 1999). Kearns indicates that the descriptive and how-to literature does not adequately address nonprofit accountability from managerial, conceptual, and policymaking standpoints. Other studies focus on narrower accountability topics, such as outcomes measurement, board governance (Ben-Ner and Van Hoomissen, 1994), financial disclosure, and fulfillment of certain tax-exempt reporting requirements to government (Chisolm, 1995).

Paton, Foote, and Payne's study (1999) of quality management standards and self-assessment approaches to accountability indicates a gap in the literature related to internally driven organizational accountability responses. Bell and Brown (1997) find that the domain of mandatory self-regulation is also lacking any significant empirical evidence about its effectiveness as an accountability approach. The literature that does exist is of a customer satisfaction orientation and does not address larger organizational and industry outcomes. There is also limited and mixed evidence about externally imposed accountability mandates and related effects on organizational performance, organizational change, and social impact (Perrin, 1998). Recent studies suggest that accountability mandates might even have a detrimental effect on the operations of nonprofits. For example, Milosfsky and Blades (1991) find that external mandates might move an organization away from its stated mission and limit stakeholder involvement in decision making. Similarly, some researchers have expressed concern that nonprofits, lacking adequate internal capacity to respond to external accountability demands, might direct their organizational energies toward meeting external accountabilities rather than toward effective change efforts (Edwards and Hulme, 1996b). Underlying this discussion is the assumption that accountability mandates will stimulate organizational performance and strengthen the investments of institutional funders. The literature does not yet provide definitive or adequate insight into these questions.

Although current research provides initial analytical and empirical tools, serious gaps persist in the literature. Recent literature tends to fall into two categories: (1) descriptive literature concerned with accountability and advocating for or against various approaches to increasing or enhancing accountability and (2) empirical literature often gathered through case studies of individual nonprofit organizations or subsector studies. Although recent case studies and other empirical work inform knowledge of accountability processes, such studies are limited in number and scope. What is missing are comprehensive case studies or empirical work related to sectorwide self-regulation initiatives. Particularly striking is the absence of data on nonprofit accountability in relationship to the public purposes of the nonprofit sector. The literature addressing accountability tends to focus on internal accountability systems, which are often idiosyncratic to specific subsectors or individual organizations. In addition, the limited rigorous research fails to illuminate adequately the debate surrounding the two primary competing approaches to accountability: mandatory self-regulation and discretionary self-regulation. Although this chapter does not propose to settle this long-standing debate, analysis of the experiences and outcomes of nonprofits participating in the review process by the Charities Review Council provides an interesting case to illuminate one statewide landscape of nonprofit accountability.

Accountability in Minnesota: Work of the Charities Review Council

The council is an independent nonprofit organization founded by citizens with a mission "to promote informed giving by donors who support charities that solicit funds in Minnesota" (CRC, 1998b, p. 3). It exercises its mission by developing a set of accountability standards, reviewing nonprofits against the standards, and making the results of the reviews available to the public. The accountability standards have been revised numerous times over the course of the council's fifty-five-year existence, with the most recent revision spanning 1996–1997. The council describes the accountability standards as "indicators of effective, ethical and accountable management practices" (CRC, 1998a, p. 1). The standards address four areas of management practice: public disclosure, governance, financial activity, and fundraising. (A full listing of the council's accountability standards can be found at http://crcmn.org/standards. The Web site includes background information on the philosophy underlying each standard.)

The council tracks the number and nature of inquiries from the public, donors, and the media regarding the operations of nonprofit organizations and initiates reviews based on public interest and, at times, public concern. It also conducts reviews, as its resources allow, at the request of individual nonprofit organizations. The council gathers information on nonprofit organizations operating in Minnesota from data compiled from the attorney general's office, various donors, and the charity itself to determine compliance with the council's standards. Its review policies specify procedures designed to foster due process and consistency of review processes. The council uses its library of information gathered from reviews to offer a variety of services targeted to several constituencies.

The council provides the following services to citizens, members of the media, researchers, nonprofit organizations, and individual and institutional donors:

- Individual, in-depth reports on some three hundred nonprofit organizations
- A database of nearly seven thousand nonprofits registered to solicit in Minnesota with information derived from public and secondary data sources
- Educational activities such as training seminars related to nonprofit accountability issues
- Publications including a periodic giving guide, which lists the results of the council's reviews
- Customized information services

The council receives its financial support from a broad base of individuals, United Ways, corporations, and foundations. Its board of directors comprises community representatives, nonprofit leaders, nonprofit consulting attorneys and accountants, and institutional donors.

Although the council relies on the voluntary participation of individual nonprofits under review, it is often referred to by the moniker of *watchdog*. As such, it is characterized as a mandatory self-regulation model by its existence as an external actor providing an accountability monitoring function. The council provides consequences in the form of public reporting that serves to reward or sanction nonprofits for their adoption and implementation of accountability practices. In contrast, the MCN's *Principles and Practices for Nonprofit Excellence* (1998) serves as an example of a discretionary self-regulation model, a set of guidelines for best practices in which internal organizational mechanisms of nonprofits drive the adoption and implementation of the suggested accountability practices. An interesting characteristic of Minnesota's nonprofit landscape centers on the degree of cooperation and consistency that exists between the two approaches: a cross-section of nonprofit and philanthropic leaders, including representatives from the council, worked together to create *Principles and Practices*; *Principles and Practices* incorporates but extends beyond the council's accountability standards; and the council and the MCN have collaborated on educational initiatives related to nonprofit accountability. In addition, the council initiated the Minnesota Nonprofit Accountability Collaborative, a working committee of leaders from the MCN, the Charities Review Council, the Office of the Minnesota Attorney General, the Management Assistance Program for Nonprofits (a Minnesota-based management support center), the Minnesota Society of Certified Public Accountants, and the Internal Revenue Service (IRS). Although the work of nonprofit regulation by the state, nonprofit advocacy by MCN, and nonprofit monitoring by the council serve unique and separate functions by purpose and design, these nonprofit regulatory and self-regulatory mechanisms operate in symbiosis in Minnesota's nonprofit sector.

Evaluation and research framework

The primary mandate of the council is the review of nonprofit organizations operating in Minnesota. Its work is also guided by the following outcome: nonprofit organizations will be strengthened by operation within a framework of industry accountability, effectiveness, and ethical operations. The evaluation study undertaken by the council was designed in part to measure this outcome for its ongoing organizational improvement and United Way reporting requirements.

The study was oriented by the overarching evaluation question: Does the review process of the council affect the operations of the nonprofit organizations reviewed? If so, how? In addition, the council was interested in feedback regarding attitudes about its recently revised accountability standards, review processes, and the quality of interactions with the council by nonprofit organizations.

The study also explored the interrelationship of internal management practices such as continuous improvement and organizational learning with external accountability demands.

Methodology

The study was oriented by both summative and formative evaluation approaches and used survey methodology. A self-designed written questionnaire was mailed to all agencies reviewed by the council during 1998 and 1999, the two years during which recently revised accountability standards were in operation. The sample size was 102: 73 agencies meeting standards and 29 agencies not meeting standards. The return of 63 surveys represents a 62 percent response rate and includes 60 agencies meeting all standards and 3 agencies not meeting all standards. Because most of the nonrespondents were agencies not meeting standards, a nonresponse study and interviews with such agencies are warranted. It will be important for the council to understand better the effects of the review process on agencies that are not operating in compliance with accountability standards. The responses of such organizations might also provide insight into the larger research themes discussed in this chapter. An additional limitation relates to potential positive and self-report bias effects at play in the study.

The primary job categories of the respondents were as follows: chief executive officers (CEOs), 65 percent; fundraising professionals, 15 percent; board chairs, 6 percent; chief financial officers, 6 percent; "other," 6 percent; and chief operating officers, 2 percent. The high response rate by CEOs and fundraising professionals corresponds with those staff members generally involved with the council review process. This suggests that the respondents are well acquainted with the review process. Although a diversity of nonprofits is represented in the sample, the majority of respondent organizations are health and human service providers.

Analysis of quantitative data centers primarily on the use of descriptive statistics. Analysis and interpretation of qualitative data from open-ended questions used an inductively generated coding scheme developed from a thorough reading of narrative responses.

Results

In terms of review processes and interactions with the council during the review process, participating nonprofits find the council's review process to be fair, objective, and appropriate. Respondents also report council staff to be responsive, fair, and talented. Many leverage the review and share results with staff, board, and funders, particularly with funders who require or request such information. A number of respondents indicated that too few donors know about or use the council's services, making the review process not as meaningful or useful as it might be. In terms of the council's review process contributing to changes in the operations of reviewed agencies, the responses are generally positive. When operational changes are reported, they are significant and well defined. A strong majority of participating nonprofits indicated that the review process increased their understanding of and commitment to accountability. Specific results follow:

- Why do nonprofits agree to be reviewed? The primary reasons for agreeing to be reviewed center on commitment to accountability (82 percent), public relations (74 percent), and self-improvement (66 percent). Secondary reasons include interest in the results of the review for self-improvement or external evaluation purposes (44 percent) and interest by key internal and external stakeholders, including corporations and foundations (38 percent), individual donors (35 percent), boards of directors (25 percent), and United Ways (15 percent). Because one of the council's standards relates to public disclosure, one respondent indicated feeling compelled to respond.
- Are the reviews burdensome? A common concern expressed by the council's board and staff, and a common criticism of mandatory self-regulation models more generally, relates to the time and resource intensities required of nonprofits being reviewed. This concern is magnified in the light of the multiple reporting obligations that nonprofits face. Ninety-four percent of participating

nonprofits indicated that the type of information that the council required was appropriate; 87 percent indicated that both the amount of information required and the time allowed for responding to the council's request for information were appropriate. Several respondents described the council's financial efficiency standard to be inappropriate due to their particular fundraising challenges or allocation of expenses related to volunteer recruitment and special events.

Several institutional factors, such as size and age, may account for the generally positive assessment of the council's review requirements. The council generally reviews organizations that have been in existence for three or more years and have annual operating budgets in excess of $350,000. Many of the nonprofits it reviews are mandated by law to conduct an annual financial audit, report annually with the state, and produce an IRS Form 990. In addition, the council conducted a series of workshops throughout the state related to the review requirements. Training initiatives and technical assistance provided to complement the review process appear to mitigate perceptions that the review process is burdensome.

In 1999, the council entered into a strategic alliance with NCIB. Instead of reviewing national organizations as it had in the past, the council will rely on NCIB's reviews instead. This may also contribute to low perceptions of redundancy because most Minnesota-based nonprofits are not routinely subjected to an additional review by national monitoring agencies.

• How do nonprofits share the results of the review? Most respondents report voluntarily sharing review results with their boards of directors (77 percent) and staff (59 percent); almost one-third share results with their volunteers (28 percent). They also share reviews with funders, typically at their request, including corporations and foundations (41 percent), individual donors (36 percent), and United Ways (20 percent). An additional 12 percent share the results with other watchdog agencies such as NCIB or PAS, or their parent or umbrella organizations.

• What are the general outcomes of the review? A large number of respondents (98 percent) indicated that it is important to meet the council's accountability standards. Several respondents indicated that the review results were important for public relations and for reinforcing their status as "accountable organizations." Most (65 percent) indicate that participation in the review process increased their organizational understanding of and commitment to nonprofit accountability. Most (59 percent) indicated that the review accurately measured and had a positive effect on their organization. Several themes emerged in the narrative responses and include affirmation of current management practices, increased confidence in operations and accountability of individual nonprofits, reinforcement of the importance of public disclosure and public trust in the nonprofit sector, increased credibility with funders, enhanced engagement by boards of directors in accountability discussions, and obtaining useful technical assistance. Several respondents indicated that the review process had value because it served as a "seal of approval" and "an external review by an independent agency." Three respondents indicated frustration that the review process was relatively unknown by their constituents. Further study is advisable to explore more fully how these results relate to internally driven review mechanisms. Are external motivations consistent with internal motivations? Do espoused organizational values in terms of the importance of accountability relate to demonstrated accountability practices?

• Do reviews lead to changes in operational practices? Respondents reported making changes in the following areas as a result of the review process: strategic planning, 13 percent; financial management, 17 percent; fundraising, 22 percent; management, 28 percent; governance, 36 percent; and communications, 35 percent. A number of respondents noted that no changes in their operations were warranted because they were already operating in compliance with standards. The number of reviewed nonprofits reporting changes is striking in the light of the fact that virtually all of the respondents were deemed to meet standards. When changes in operational practices did occur, the changes were specific and centered on fundraising and administrative cost containment, policy improvement such as adopting conflict of interest and fundraising guidelines, consistent accounting for special events, and improved disclosure. In addition, a number of respondents reported that the review process increased board involvement with and knowledge of accountability. Few respondents saw the review process as being tied to or leading to changes in strategic planning efforts.

• Does the review process further outcomes goals? In terms of the review process reinforcing a nonprofit's outcomes goals, the results are mixed: approximately 55 percent of respondents agreed or strongly agreed that the council's review reinforced outcomes goals, and 45 percent indicated disagreement or strong disagreement. Nearly 10 percent did not respond or indicated that they did not have outcomes goals. The narrative responses (although limited in number) indicate that many agencies view the review process as having utility in terms of reinforcing their outcomes only to the extent that the improvement of general operations or management practices is directly tied to achieving outcomes results. Generally, there is a wide variety of interpretations of the term *outcomes.* Review agencies will need to define such terms better to gain further insight into these processes.

• What internally driven accountability responses are at play? Participating nonprofits employ a number of internal accountability mechanisms, including financial audits, 84 percent; internal outcomes evaluation, 63 percent; internal organizational review process, 62 percent; board self-evaluation, 61 percent; and ongoing improvement initiatives related to results from external outcomes evaluation, 42 percent. In addition, 84 percent of respondents report adherence to a set of discretionary self-regulation standards. Specifically, 49 percent of participating nonprofits report abiding by the council on Nonprofits Principles and Practices for Nonprofit Excellence; 33 percent report that their professional fundraising staff subscribes to the code of ethics of the National Society of Fundraising Executives. It is not surprising that these nonprofits also actively engage in public disclosure activities by making the following routinely available to donors: IRS Form 990, 93 percent; annual report, 88 percent; financial audit, 83 percent; and review by the council, 64 percent. Routine sharing of results from internal evaluations, external evaluations, and review by other watchdog agencies occurs in less than 25 percent of the participating nonprofits. It is noteworthy that 7 percent of organizations reported not routinely providing Form 990 despite the legal requirement to do so.

• Who provides organizational leadership on accountability? In participating nonprofits with budgets less than $1.5 million, the following parties provide leadership on accountability: 89 percent of smaller organizations reported that the CEO provides leadership; 75 percent indicated the board of directors as providing leadership; 50 percent indicated leadership by program directors; 29 percent indicated fundraising staff; 25 percent indicated leadership board chair; 16 percent indicated the fundraising director; 18 percent the marketing staff; and 7 percent the marketing director. In participating nonprofits with budgets equal to or greater than $1.5 million, the following parties provide leadership on accountability: 93 percent of larger organizations reported that the CEO provides leadership; 85 percent reported that the board of directors provides leadership; 58 percent indicated the board chair provides leadership; 54 percent indicated leadership by program directors; 45 percent indicated fundraising staff; 42 percent indicated the fundraising director; 24 percent indicated the marketing director; and 18 percent indicated marketing staff. When considering the participating nonprofits by budget size, a significant difference was found in the area of leadership being provided by board chairs and fundraising directors: larger organizations more frequently indicated that fundraising directors and board chairs provide leadership on accountability. These areas of significance may be explained by a focus on board development and governance in larger organizations or the use of more sophisticated and indirect forms of fundraising, such as telemarketing and direct mail, which may require a heightened accountability focus and, consequently, a higher degree of leadership on accountability related activities.

• How do donors use review information? Based on the survey of reviewed nonprofits, 36 percent reported sharing review results with individual donors; 41 percent reported sharing results with foundations and corporations. A question remains as to how donors use the review information. Since 1994, the council has conducted an annual survey of individual donors. Although not based on a statistically valid sample, results have been largely consistent throughout this period, with 1997 results from a survey of 197 randomly selected individuals who had previously used the council's review information. These annual surveys provide some insight through several emergent trends:

> 55% of respondents indicated that the Council's telephone information services were very helpful in their giving decisions; 36% indicated that Council's telephone services were helpful in their giving decisions.
>
> 60% of respondents indicated that the Council's written publications were very helpful in their giving decisions; 26% indicated that that the Council's written publications were helpful in their giving decisions.
>
> 94% of respondents indicated that "services provided by the Charities Review Council helped me make better informed giving decisions" [CRC, 1998a].

In the light of the challenges of obtaining a statistically significant return and in an effort to gain new insight, in 2000 the council undertook a small-scale process of in-depth telephone interviews with donors who use their services. Exploratory in nature and not generalizable, these interviews do suggest that respondents found the council's services useful in informing their charitable giving activities, had a desire to be and to feel informed in their decision making on charitable giving, and expressed limited personal time to do independent research and, as a result, relied on the council for information.

The 2000 interviews also mirror results that emerged from the council's 1996 Donor's Jury (CRC, 1996), a public hearing about the work of the council: that individual donors find summary reports appealing and financial measures useful. In the 2000 study, donors indicated the following motivations for donating: financial efficiency, the mission of the nonprofit, whether the nonprofit meets the council's standards, their own familiarity with a nonprofit organization, and good board governance. When queried about the appropriateness of pursuing reviews that would include effectiveness criteria, the respondents indicated that they would like to see effectiveness reports, but several acknowledged the potential complexities of such an approach. Much like the nonprofit survey data reported in the next section, some confusion emerged regarding the meaning of effectiveness, with several respondents associating it with financial efficiency or donations being used for "the cause of charities." The council indicates that it will continue to pursue alternative evaluation methods in an effort to gain a better understanding of the needs of donors. This will be important as it tries to meet the needs of its various constituencies, respond to changes in the philanthropic environment, and broaden the audiences it serves.

• Should the standards be expanded to include effectiveness criteria? In the past five years, the council, NCIB, and PAS have all undertaken large-scale processes to study and revise their respective standards. The issue of adding effectiveness criteria surfaced during these examinations. In addition, "much of the accountability discussion in the practitioner literature and in various electronic discussion groups indicates that many focus on financial accountability to the exclusion of other measures, such as effectiveness" (R. Cowles, personal communication, Apr. 20, 2001). The council was concerned not only about repeated calls for effectiveness criteria, but also by the possibility that its constituents, particularly individual donors, perceived that its standards currently address issues of effectiveness. The standards in fact are more oriented toward efficiency and transparency criteria and do not overtly address issues of organizational effectiveness. The council wished to explore the perspectives of nonprofits related to the addition of such criteria.

Seventy-one percent of participating nonprofits expressed disagreement with the proposition that the council add effectiveness criteria to its standards. Several nonprofits, however, designated specific effectiveness criteria as needing to be added to the standards in such areas as outcomes, entrepreneurship, and pluralism. Similar to the discussion of outcomes, review agencies will need to define effectiveness criteria and then conduct further research. For example, it might be useful for review agencies to explore feedback on several scenarios for how effectiveness reviews could be carried out, such as multiattribute utility evaluations, cost-benefit analyses, and a voluntary effectiveness review component. It will be important for review agencies to seek the perspectives of donors as well as nonprofits in relationship to these issues.

- How do internal organizational practices relate to external accountability processes? In the Minnesota context, the evaluation study suggests that more than 60 percent of organizations are engaged in some sort of internal self-study process. More than 50 percent embrace voluntary standards such as MCN's *Principles and Practices for Nonprofit Excellence.* In addition, the study revealed that leadership of accountability initiatives occurs at various board and staff levels, with strong trends (in excess of 80 percent) reporting both board chair and CEO involvement. Adoption of professional codes of ethics or voluntary standards and development of an internal ethos of self-improvement and reflection emerge as self-directed responses to external accountability demands.

Table 4.2 illustrates organizational practices associated with continuous improvement and organizational learning paradigms and proposes areas related to internally driven accountability practices.[2] The case of Minnesota suggests that processes of organizational learning and continuous improvement may be at play in high levels of both internal and external accountability implementation. Accountability responses do not, however, appear to be tied to long-term or strategic planning. This is an area in need of further exploration.

Future research

The study's findings suggest that (1) nonprofits need sufficient capacity to respond to external accountability demands, part of which may be related to the adoption of internal accountability capacities; (2) capacity-building initiatives designed to strengthen internal accountability responses associated with continuous improvement and organizational learning would be useful; and (3) there may be a discrepancy between espoused accountability beliefs, internally driven or discretionary forms of self-regulation in current use, and efforts to meet externally driven or mandatory forms of self-regulation. The study's findings are tentative in nature but suggest areas warranting additional research.

The Minnesota case also suggests that mandatory self-regulation models are strengthened when nonprofits are provided tools or capacity for changing: how to implement accountability practices must be made explicit. Training and technical assistance efforts oriented around accountability practices appear useful. Mandatory initiatives cannot assume that nonprofits will know how to develop internal accountability capacity simply through general services provided by management support centers, generic nonprofit training initiatives, or good governance. Within a context of mandatory self-regulation, organizations can build internal accountability capacity sufficient to foster the implementation of accountability practices, especially when a symbiosis of local resources and accountability initiatives exists. Similarly, reforms involving OL/CI are also well aligned with the development of strong internal accountability capacity, in part because such practices build organizational capacity specific to accountability needs and may also contribute to the development of an ethos of internally driven accountability. In short, internal accountability capacity and external accountability initiatives can be reinforcing and additive versus being either in conflict or redundant. The council states the following core belief: "The responsible actions both of donors and of charities will sustain and enhance the climate for charitable giving" (CRC, 1997, p. 2). Although this belief is not yet well supported empirically, the complementary and reinforcing nature of mandatory and discretionary forms of self-regulation can be expressed in similar form: the responsible actions of both watchdogs and nonprofits will sustain and enhance the climate for nonprofit accountability. Further research is needed, however, to determine the extent to which this proposition is valid.

Table 4.2. A comparison of continuous improvement (CI) and organizational learning (OL) practices with nonprofit accountability practices

Organizational Practice Areas	*Continuous Improvement*	*Organizational Learning*	*Related Nonprofit Practices*
Visions and Goals	Collective vision; clear goals are implied.	There are no set goals, but there is a collective vision.	Accountability goals or vision are shared throughout the organization.
Organizational Processes	Study organizational processes.	Study and learn about every aspect of organizational functioning.	Organizations are engaged in self-study about processes and results related to accountability; this study is approached systemically.
Epistemology and Research or Assessment Approaches	Causal analysis and scientific method are the basis for using data for decision making.	Accepts broader perspectives on truth and methods.	Evaluation is employed. Alternative forms of inquiry and data are used and valued.
Constituency Orientation	Focus on customers' needs is primary to improving quality.	Not stated.	Accountability concerns are viewed in the context of internal and external stakeholder needs.
Resource Orientation	Improvements ought to be possible without additional resources.	Not stated.	Accountability improvement is possible with existing financial or human resources.
Self-Assessment and Reflection	Not stated.	Learning from the past is important; reflection and reflective dialogue.	There is evidence of self-study and reflective practice at the individual and organizational levels.
Collaboration	Collaboration is necessary for an effective organization.	Collaboration is required to turn "facts" into commonly agreed-on knowledge.	Collaboration contributes to opportunities to learn about accountability
Orientation to Change; long-term v. short-term	Improvement requires a long-term focus.	Not stated but implied.	Accountability initiatives are built into long-term planning, not simply conducted on a one-time or as-needed basis.

Table 4.2. *(continued)*

Organizational Practice Areas	*Continuous Improvement*	*Organizational Learning*	*Related Nonprofit Practices*
Internal Modes of Authority; hierarchical v. participatory	Staff and board involvement acrosslevels in levels in organization are engaged in decision making, and resources devoted to staff development are central.	Staff- and board-held knowledge is critical for organizational improvement.	Knowledge related to accountability should be held at various board, staff, and volunteer levels.
Individual/ Collective Elements	CI can occur as a consequence of both individual and group work.	OL occurs only in social contexts.	Accountability can occur in social contexts or as a consequence of individual and group work. Accountability initiatives should not just stop with one department or one individual to be effective.
Intentionality/ Planning	CI is a conscious element of organizational procedure.	OL may be planned or unplanned.	Accountability occurs at two levels, conscious or planned, and unplanned or responsive to changing circumstances. This considers a link between espoused values and demonstrated accountability practices.

Source: Adapted from Ingram et al. (1999) to nonprofit organizational aspects. Used by permission.

Future research is also warranted to examine the proposed link between (1) continuous improvement, organizational learning, and development of strong internal accountability capacity and (2) strong internal capacity as serving to facilitate the implementation of accountability practices. Several research questions emerge from this study that might also help explain why the extent of accountability implementation varies among nonprofits and how such variance might be associated with nonprofits that have strong continuous improvement and organizational learning practices:

What internal organizational factors relate to the ability of a nonprofit organization to respond to externally imposed accountability policies? What capacity-building activities or resources facilitate responsiveness to accountability policies?

Are nonprofit organizations that employ continuous improvement and organizational learning practices better able to develop strong internal accountability capacity? Are nonprofit organizations that employ continuous improvement and organizational learning practices better able to respond to external accountability mandates? What continuous improvement and organizational learning related tools and or practices support these circumstances?

Research designed to respond to these questions promises to inform understanding of the interaction between internal organizational practices and accountability practices. Insight into this relationship may strengthen nonprofit management capacity and the effective and ethical operations of both mandatory and discretionary self-regulation initiatives.

Notes

1. The National Charities Information Bureau and the Council of Better Business Bureaus' Foundation, which houses the Philanthropic Advisory Service program, have merged. The name of the merged organization is the BBB Wise Giving Alliance. The alliance employs a set of published standards to review the activities of selected charities and announces the results in press releases, through published reports and on its web site at http://www.give.org.

2. For a parallel discussion of OL/CI practices within education, see Leithwood and Cousins (1998). Duffy (1997) and Marks, Louis, and Guerrera (1999) provide useful discussion of OL/CI practices in the context of educational accountability and performance improvement efforts. In addition, Mulford (1998) explores OL/CI practices in relationship to change processes in education. Newmann, King, and Rigdon (1997) present a useful framework for accountability systems currently in use in education.

References

Argyris, C., & Schön, D. *Theory in Practice: Increasing Professional Effectiveness.* San Francisco: Jossey-Bass, 1974.

Argyris, C., & Schön, D. *Organizational Learning II: Theory, Method, and Practice.* Reading, MA: Addison-Wesley, 1996.

Bell, C., and Brown, R. D. "Accountability Enforcement by Oversight Groups." In D. L. Kurtz (ed.), *New York University's Twenty-Fifth Conference on Tax Planning for 501(c)(3) Organizations.* New York: Matthew-Bender, 1997.

Ben-Ner, A., and Van Hoomissen, T. "The Governance of Nonprofit Organizations: Law and Public Policy." *Nonprofit Management and Leadership,* 1994, *4,* 393–414.

Bothwell, R. O. "Trends in Self-Regulation and Transparency of Nonprofits in the U.S." *International Journal of Not-for-Profit Law,* 1999. http://www.icnl.org/journal/vol2iss3/Arn_bothwell.htm

Charities Review Council. *Donor's Jury Proceedings.* St. Paul, Minn.: Charities Review Council, 1996.

Charities Review Council. *1997 Annual Report to Constituents.* St. Paul, Minn.: Charities Review Council, 1997.

Charities Review Council. *Accountability Standards.* St. Paul, MN, 1998a.

Charities Review Council. *1998 Annual Report to Constituents: Sound choices, solid charities.* St. Paul, Minn.: Charities Review Council, 1998b.

Charities Review Council. *1999 Annual Report to Constituents.* St. Paul, Minn.: Charities Review Council, 1999.

Charities Review Council. *2000 Annual Report to Constituents.* St. Paul, Minn.: Charities Review Council, 2000.

Child, J. "Organizational Structure, Environment, and Performance: The Role of Strategic Choice." *Sociology,* 1972, *6,* 1–22.

Chisolm, L. B. "Accountability of Nonprofit Organizations and Those Who Control Them: The Legal Framework." *Nonprofit Management and Leadership,* 1995, *6,* 141–156.

Deming, W. E. *Out of the Crisis.* Cambridge, MA: MIT Center for Advanced Engineering Study, 1986.

Detert, J.R., Kopel, M.B., Mauriel, J. and Jenni, R. Quality Management in U.S. High Schools: Evidence from the Field. *Journal of School Leadership, 10* (March), 2000, 158-187.

DiMaggio, P. J., and Powell, W. W. "The Iron Cage Revisited: Institutional Isomorphism and Collective Rationality in Organizational Fields." *American Sociological Review,* 1983, *48,* 47–60.

Drucker, P.F. *Managing for Results: Economic Tasks and Risk-Taking Decisions.* New York: Harper & Row, 1964.

Duffy, F. M. "Knowledge Work Supervision: Transforming School Systems into High Performing Learning Organizations." *International Journal of Educational Management,* 1997, *11,* 26–31.

Edwards, M. "Organizational Learning in Non-Governmental Organizations: What Have We Learned?" *Public Administration and Development,* 17, 1997, 235-250.

Edwards, M., and Hulme, D. *Making a Difference: NGOs and Development in a Changing World.* London: Earthscan, 1992.

Edwards, M., and Hulme, D. *Beyond the Magic Bullet: NGO Performance and*

Accountability in the Post Cold War World. West Hartford, Conn.: Kumarian Press, 1996a.

Edwards, M., and Hulme, D. "Too Close for Comfort? The Impact of Official Aid on Nongovernmental Organizations." *World Development*, 1996b, *24*, 961–973.

Eisenberg, P. "A Crisis in the Nonprofit Sector." *National Civic Review*, 1997, *86*, 331–341.

Estes, C., Biney, E. A., and Bergthold, L. "How the Legitimacy of the Sector Has Eroded." In V. Hodgkinson and others (eds.), *The Future of the Nonprofit Sector.* San Francisco: Jossey-Bass, 1989.

Fowler, A. (1997). *Striking a Balance: A Guide to the Management of NGOs.* London: Earthscan.

Gilley, J.W., and Maycunich, A. *Organizational Learning, Performance, and Change: An Introduction to Strategic Human Resource Development.* Cambridge, MA: Perseus, 2000.

Hall, P. D. "Abandoning the Rhetoric of Independence: Reflections on the Nonprofit Sector in the Post-Liberal Era." In S. A. Ostrander, S. Langston, and J. Van Til (eds.), *Shifting the Debate: Public/Private Sector Relations in the Modern Welfare State.* New Brunswick, N.J.: Transaction Books, 1987.

Hammack, D. C. "Accountability and Nonprofit Organizations: A Historical Perspective." *Nonprofit Management and Leadership*, 1995, *6*, 127–139.

Handy, C.B. *Understanding Organizations.* New York: Oxford University Press, 1993.

Hannan, M. T., and Freeman, J. "The Population Ecology of Organizations." *American Journal of Sociology*, 1977, *82*, 929–964.

Hannan, M. T., and Freeman, J. "Structural Inertia and Organizational Change." *American Sociological Review*, 1984, *49*, 149–164.

INDEPENDENT SECTOR. *Why Should INDEPENDENT SECTOR Focus on Accountability?* Washington, D.C.: INDEPENDENT SECTOR, 2000.

Ingram, D., Louis, K. S., & Schroeder, R. G. Louis. *Data-Based Decision-Making in U.S. High Schools.* Presentation at the Annual Meeting of the American Educational Research Association in Montreal, Quebec, Canada, April, 1999.

Juran, J.M. *Juran on Planning for Quality.* New York: Free Press, 1988.

Kearns, K. "The Strategic Management of Accountability in Nonprofit Organizations: An Analytical Framework." *Public Administration Review*, 1994, *54*, 185–192.

Kearns, K. *Managing for Accountability.* San Francisco: Jossey-Bass, 1996.

Lawry, R. P. "Accountability and Nonprofit Organizations: An Ethical Perspective." *Nonprofit Management and Leadership*, 1995, *6*, 171–180.

Leithwood, K., and Louis, K. S. *Organizational Learning in Schools.* Lisse, NL: Swets and Zeitlinger, 1996.

Letts, C.W., Ryan, W.P., and Grossman, A.S. *High Performance Nonprofit Organizations: Managing Upstream for Greater Impact.* New York: John Wiley, 1999.

Light, P. C. *Making Nonprofits Work.* Washington, D.C.: Brookings Institution, 2000.

Marks, H. M., Louis, K. S., and Guerrera, S. "The Capacity for Organizational Learning: Implications for Pedagogical Quality and Student Achievement." Paper presented at the annual meeting of the American Educational Research Association, Montreal, Quebec, Canada, Apr. 1999.

Meyer, J. W., and Rowan, B. "Institutionalized Organizations: Formal Structure as Myth and Ceremony." *American Journal of Sociology*, 1977, *83*, 340–363.

Miller, D., and Friesen, P. *Organizations: A Quantum View*. Upper Saddle River, N.J.: Prentice-Hall, 1984.

Milosfsky, C., and Blades, S. D. "Issues of Accountability in Health Charities: A Case Study of Accountability Problems Among Nonprofit Organizations." *Nonprofit and Voluntary Sector Quarterly*, 1991, *20*, 371–372, 378.

Minnesota Council of Nonprofits. *Principles and Practices for Nonprofit Excellence*. St. Paul, MN: MCN, 1998.

Minnesota Council if Nonprofits. *Minnesota Nonprofit Economy Report*. St. Paul, Minn.: Minnesota Council of Nonprofits, 2001. http://www.mncn.org/np_econ.htm

Mintzberg, H. *The Structuring of Organizations*. Upper Saddle River, N.J.: Prentice-Hall, 1979.

Mintzberg, H. "Organization Design: Fit or Fashion?" *Harvard Business Review*, 1981, *59*, 103–116.

Mulford, W. "Organizational Learning and Educational Change." In A. Hargreaves, A. Lieberman, M. Fullan, and D. Hopkins (eds.), *International Handbook of Educational Change*. Norwell. Mass.: Kluwer, 1998.

National Charities Information Bureau. *Standards in Philanthropy*. New York: National Charities Information Bureau, 1996.

Newmann, F., King, B. M., and Rigdon, M. "Accountability and School Performance: Implications from Restructuring Schools." *Harvard Educational Review*, 1997, *67*, 41–74.

Paton, R., Foote, J., and Payne, G. "What Happens When Nonprofits Use Quality Models for Self-Assessment?" *Nonprofit Management and Leadership*, 1999, *20*, 21–34.

Perrin, B. "Effective Use And Misuse of Performance Measurement." *American Journal of Evaluation*, 1998, *19*, 367–379.

Pfeffer, J., and Salancik, G. *The External Control of Organizations*. New York: HarperCollins, 1978.

Pratt, J. "The Case of Minnesota: Institutionalizing Public Spirit." In E. Clotfelter and T. Ehrlich (eds.), *Philanthropy and the Nonprofit Sector in a Changing America*. Bloomington: Indiana University Press, 1999.

Schene, P. M. "Accountability in Nonprofit Organizations: A Framework for Addressing the Public Interest." Unpublished doctoral dissertation, University of Colorado at Denver, 1991.

Scott, W. R. *Institutions and Organizations*. Thousand Oaks, Calif.: Sage, 1995.

Swanson, R.A., and Houlton, E. *Results: How to Assess Performance, Learning, and Perceptions in Organizations*. San Francisco: Berrett-Koehler, 1999.

Williamson, O. E. *Markets and Hierarchies: Analysis and Anti-Trust Implications*. New York: Free Press, 1975.

Williamson, O. E. "The Modern Corporation: Origin, Evolution, Attributes." *Journal of Economic Literature*, 1981, *19*, 1537–1568.

Williamson, O. E. *The Economic Institutions of Capitalism.* New York: Free Press, 1985.
Zucker, L. G. "Organizations as Institutions." In B. Shaw (ed.), *Research in the Sociology of Organizations* (Vol. 2) Greenwich, Conn.: JAI Press, 1983.
Zucker, L. G. "Institutional Theories of Organization." *Annual Review of Sociology,* 1987, *13,* 443–464.

ANGELA L. BIES *is a member of the public administration faculty at Texas A & M University. She is a comparative researcher who focuses on ethics, accountability, organizational capacity, and evaluation in nonprofit/nongovernmental organizations. Angela held several nonprofit leadership positions prior to serving in a research and teaching role.*

Ultimately, nonprofits are accountable to members of the public as they are enjoy the benefits of tax-exempt status and receive tax-deductible donations from individuals and organizations. The National Center for Charitable Statistics describes its efforts to provide more high quality data on charities that will help give researchers, policymakers, and the public the ability to assess the impact and increase the accountability of these organizations.

5

Nonprofit accountability and the National Center for Charitable Statistics

Thomas H. Pollak, Linda M. Lampkin

"YOU GAVE ME—entrusted me—with a hundred dollars. I have used it wisely to make a better world, and this is what I accomplished as a result." These two sentences capture the essence of what it means for nonprofit organizations, or the sector as a whole, to be accountable. Being accountable implies that one is responsible for one's actions, is answerable to some higher authority (primarily donors, but also, to some extent, the general public and the beneficiaries of the organization's services), and can give an accounting of one's actions.

Sometimes these accounts may be quite general, such as, "You gave me a hundred dollars, and I fed, clothed, and housed a homeless person." More often, the outputs and the outcomes are measured: "You gave me a hundred dollars, and we spent twenty dollars to purchase groceries, ten dollars for a used winter coat, and the remaining seventy dollars for a security deposit on a small apartment for the homeless man. Six months later, he has found a job, is happily settled in his new apartment, and is paying his rent on time." The more specific account is much more satisfying than the general one. It captures the input (one hundred dollars), the output (how the money was used), as well as the outcomes or results ("Six months later . . ."). The National Center for Charitable Statistics (NCCS) at the Urban Institute is helping to build both the data and methodological framework to enable this type of accountability in the nonprofit sector.

Efforts in the early 1970s to better understand the nonprofit sector culminated in the report of the Commission on Private Philanthropy and Public Needs (known as the Filer Commission) in 1975. With members from foundations and other nonprofit representatives, the goals of this privately established commission were to study and make recommendations about philanthropic institutions in the United States. The report laid the groundwork for the creation of Independent Sector (IS) and NCCS by calling for better quality data and more information on the sector (Brilliant, 2000). Founded by a number of nonprofit scholars, practitioners, NCCS was a program of the IS research division until 1996 when it moved to the Urban Institute, a nonprofit, nonpartisan research organization.

NCCS serves as a repository of data on the nonprofit sector, working to develop new sources of data and to use the data to measure the size and scope of the sector. But there was work to be done initially on building the infrastructure to measure the economic activities of the nonprofit sector. This included developing a standard classification system (the National Taxonomy of Exempt Entities, or NTEE, now used by the Internal Revenue Service, as well as by most nonprofit researchers and practitioners) as well as collecting data from a variety of sources. *Dimensions of the Independent*

Sector and its successor, *The Nonprofit Almanac*, compiled data from a variety of sources such as the U.S. Census Bureau's Economic Census (conducted every five years), IRS Statistics of Income Division's organization samples, the Foundation Center, and other sources to provide a more complete portrait of the sector. (Other IS research publications such as *Giving and Volunteering* and *From Belief to Commitment* broadened the focus to include analyses of households' charitable giving, volunteering, and the activities of religious congregations, among other research areas.)

How do you measure the nonprofit sector? One approach is to collect data from the umbrella organizations, research groups, and regulators for each subsector in the nonprofit sector. For example, both the U.S. Health Care Financing Administration and the American Hospital Association collect a vast array of data on hospitals. Unfortunately, good subsector-level data tend to be found in only a few areas. Even if there were strong data collection efforts in every subsector, the amazing diversity of the sector makes this strategy problematic. (The NTEE contains more than six hundred categories ranging from arts and education to health, human services, and religion. An explanation is available at http://www.nccs.urban.org/ntee-cc/.)

Data from IRS Form 990, which most secular nonprofit organizations with more than twenty-five thousand dollars in revenues are required to file with the IRS, emerged as the key source. The form and its accompanying schedules include hundreds of items focused on organizational finances as well as data on programs, legal structure, boards, key employees, advocacy activities, and a range of other items. The detailed information on revenues, expenses, assets, and liabilities formed the core of most research by NCCS, as well as much research by others on the sector.

This chapter discusses the information that is necessary to ensuring that the nonprofit sector is accountable and the role of NCCS in developing such data. Those interested in accountability are a varied group, with different interest and data needs. We hope that an understanding of current NCCS activities and the quality of existing data, as well as more speculative and conceptual discussions about the role of accountability and the nonprofit sector, generally will help readers understand our goals and interests.

The need for better data

As researchers at IS, NCCS, Philanthropic Research Inc. (PRI), and in the academic community sought to use IRS lists of registered organizations and IRS Forms 990, a range of problems with the data were uncovered. In the late 1980s, the New York City Nonprofit Project found that 50 percent of the organizations in the IRS listing of nonprofits in New York City could not be located. Equally troubling, 50 percent of the organizations identified in the New York City census could not be found on the IRS rolls (Haycock, 1992). Although there is a range of valid reasons for some discrepancies (for example, congregations and most religious organizations need not register or file with the IRS), the magnitude of the difference raised troubling questions about the quality of the IRS listings.

The financial data reported on Form 990 has also been the object of substantial criticism. During the course of its research, IS found a number of problems with IRS data. Some were the result of errors in an IRS data entry process geared toward rapid input of key variables; others could be explained only by a lack of care shown by some organizations. These problems included missing entries, uninformative program descriptions, and arithmetic errors.

Froelich and Knoepfle (1996), in their comparison of audited financial statements with Form 990 data, found substantial discrepancies between the two sources and emphasized weaknesses in Form 990. Others have noted the surprisingly large percentage of organizations that report receiving substantial private contributions yet report zero fundraising costs (Cordes, Pollak, and Wilson, 1999). Underreporting and misreporting of fundraising costs, especially when incurred by professional fundraisers, has long been a concern of state charity officials.

Some recent studies on quality have been more encouraging (McLean and Lampkin, 1999; Froelich, Knoepfle, and Pollak, 2000), showing that the Form 990 can be considered a reliable source of financial information. The quality of the data appears to be improving with the increasing visibility of the information on the Internet through GuideStar and NCCS.

Accountability revisited

In order to understand the connection between the work of NCCS and issues of accountability better, it is first necessary to explore what is meant by the term. Public interest in accountability in the nonprofit sector tends to heighten when a case of misconduct is publicized, but the term itself can be interpreted much more broadly. Any discussion of accountability needs to recognize the many questions of interpretation. Accountable to whom? Donors or members? Beneficiaries of the organization's services? The local community, or a larger state or national interest? Some higher moral, ethical, professional, or artistic standard? (See Hammack, 1995, for a historical perspective.) Accountable for what? Not engaging in misconduct or illegal activity? Or for fulfilling the mission?

Herzlinger (1996) provides one well-crafted answer. She offers a set of four problems that nonprofit and government accountability systems are intended to address: inefficiency, ineffectiveness, private inurement, and excessive risk. However, the significance assigned to these problems varies depending on a reviewer's conception of the sector. For some, the sector is an idealized realm of passionate social entrepreneurs, civic involvement, committed volunteers, and board members. To others, the sector is the major institutions of higher education, the hospitals, and other bureaucratized organizations, characterized only by a different form of legal structure, with its employees and organizations lacking in any special virtue. These organizations are not unlike any for-profit business. If they differ, they do so because they are less accountable, less constrained by oversight by owners and stakeholders.

If one views the sector as populated by hundreds of thousands (or even millions, depending on estimates of very small organizations) of small and innovative organizations, a focus on holding organizations accountable for being efficient and effective seems misplaced. In fact, the virtue of the sector is in its creativity, energy, good intentions, and participatory role. Results are less important than process and risk taking and innovation more important than bureaucratic efficiency. On the other hand, if one focuses on the largest 4 percent of the organizations that account for about 75 percent of the sector's revenues and assets, then efficiency, effectiveness, and prudent stewardship of resources (that is, avoidance of excessive risk) become critical components of accountability.

NCCS research and data projects touch on all of the problems Herzlinger identified, although some more than others. NCCS seeks to present the media, policymakers, and the public with a balanced picture of the nonprofit sector that does justice to both dimensions of the sector—the economically dominant large institutions and the multiplicity of small organizations (see Stevenson, Pollak, and Lampkin, 1997). NCCS research generally provides separate analyses of large and small organizations, as well as distinctions by type of organizations (for example, health, human services, and environmental groups) to highlight their significant differences (Pollak and Pettit, 1997).

Of particular interest to the questions of nonprofit accountability is NCCS's work on fundraising and administrative costs. NCCS is using a combination of Form 990 data, surveys, and case studies to move beyond anecdotal evidence about fundraising abuse, "one size fits all" fundraising ratios, and speculations about inconsistent cost reporting. The goal is to create a new level of understanding in the sector about what constitutes reasonable overhead costs and to help the sector reassess the balance that has been struck between uniform reporting standards and the need to give managers and accountants flexibility.

More generally, using dissemination of data or information as a tool for accountability has a long history in the United States, dating back to support for freedom of the press as enunciated in the Federalist Papers and the First Amendment. Disclosure of data as a specific tool for accountability goes back to the Securities and Exchange Acts of 1933 and 1934 and has been employed more recently in the Federal Election Campaign Act of 1971 (governing disclosure by candidates, political action committees, and political parties engaged in federal elections), the Emergency Planning and Community Right-to-Know Act of 1996 (requiring manufacturers releasing toxic chemicals to disclose the types and amounts), and the Freedom of Information Act of 1966 (government records generally).

NCCS is working to create standards for reporting data that will allow comparisons and analyses of changes over time. Just disseminating data as an accountability tool is not enough in the nonprofit sector because of the lack of standard definitions and formats for data. For example, the use of a standard chart of accounts for nonprofit accounting would greatly enhance comparability among nonprofits. Standard types of outcome measures for similar types of organizations would also improve accountability. Only with such standards can the dissemination of data become an effective tool.

An overview of NCCS

NCCS activities can be grouped around four goals: (1) improve the quality of the data collected from the Form 990 and other current data systems, (2) broaden the range of data collection to include organizations that do not file Form 990 and data that are not on the form, (3) lower the cost of producing data, and (4) increase dissemination and use of the data.

The following sections discuss specific projects and, more generally, NCCS's approach to advancing these goals through prudent use of technology and partnerships.

Partnerships and technology

NCCS has sought to develop partnerships and exploit technology to maximize what it can accomplish. In contrast to other national statistical organizations such as the federal National Center for

Education Statistics and National Center for Health Statistics, NCCS receives no government support for its core activities.

The need for data on the nonprofit sector is shared not only by researchers but also by the IRS, grant-making foundations, government policymakers and regulators, the press, and nonprofit umbrella organizations. NCCS believes that the best way to meet its need for high-quality data is to join forces with these other stakeholders to build the information infrastructure. These partnerships include both long-term relationships with broad activities and newer project-specific alliances to accomplish specific objectives.

At the national level, NCCS partners range from nonprofit associations like IS, the National Council of Nonprofit Associations (NCNA), and the National Association of Attorneys-General/National Association of State Charity Officials (NASCO), to other data collection organizations such as PRI (with its GuideStar Web site—www.guidestar.org) and the Foundation Center, to industry-specific alliances with groups like OPERA America, the National Assembly of State Arts Agencies, and the Alliance of Information and Referral Services. Projects with the National Endowment for the Arts and the Centers for Disease Control have also been invaluable in improving and expanding data sources. At the state and local levels, NCCS has worked with a range of organizations, including the Nonprofit Coordinating Committee of New York, Donors Forum of Chicago, and the Washington Association of Grantmakers.

Technology plays an increasingly important role in creating, cleaning, analyzing, and disseminating data. The most important use of technology for NCCS's work during the past five years was not one that it made possible. NCCS contracted with the IRS to purchase scanned images of all Forms 990 filed by 501(c)(3) organizations (both public charities and private foundations) from 1996 to 2001. This contract enabled the perennially underfinanced Exempt Organizations Division of the IRS (now called the Tax Exempt and Government Entities Division) to purchase the high-speed scanners, high-volume storage systems, and CD-ROM mastering systems necessary to process, store, and electronically copy hundreds of thousands of returns and millions of pages each year. NCCS, in turn, receives several copies of the images, some of which are given to project partner PRI, which makes the images available on the Web and, working through subcontractors, keypunches hundreds of data items from each return, thus creating a research database.

The free and convenient access to hundreds of thousands of Form 990 returns through the GuideStar Web site has revolutionized the way that the press, researchers, regulators, and many donors (potential or actual) learn about the finances and, to a lesser extent, the activities of nonprofit organizations. While organizations' Forms 990 have been available on request from the IRS for many years, the nonprofit organizations themselves were required to make them conveniently available as recently as 1999. With the addition of the GuideStar Web site, a process that had previously taken four to six weeks has been reduced to a matter of minutes. This increased accessibility and visibility of Form 990 has immensely increased its usefulness as an accountability tool.

The Form 990 fields digitized include the descriptions of nonprofit programs. NCCS has taken advantage of this new source of data to create a system to classify nonprofit programs, activities, and services and then to develop a method to assign the codes by computer. This second classification system will provide a much broader view of the organization, not just its type as designated by the NTEE.

Over the past decade, NCCS, IRS, and IS have classified more than 400,000 organizations using the NTEE. For the most part, these organizations have been classified one organization at a time by IRS determination specialists (who review organizations' applications for exempt status) and by NCCS and IS research staff. This process is extremely time-consuming and fraught with error. Challenges include hiring and retaining staff interested in the detailed work of classification; the inherent complexity of working with a system that includes hundreds of categories; and incomplete, vague, or ambiguous information on organizational activities and purposes.

The automated classification system will be used to code the activities and also check the NTEE organizational type. The use of these two systems together will not solve the problem of incomplete information, but it can go a long way toward ensuring consistent classifications that accurately capture the available information.

On the horizon for NCCS is the use of "Web crawling" technology for automating the process of searching the Web for information on organizations. Use of this approach would enable data to be collected from Web sites without contacting the organizations. This could help fill gaps in knowledge of organization activities on which the Form 990 is silent.

Current projects

Other major NCCS projects range from a focus on improving the quality and lowering the cost of financial data to new and challenging efforts to measure the outcomes of nonprofit activity.

Electronic filing. NCCS is working on a pilot project with eleven state charity offices to create an electronic data repository for state charity registration that would include electronic filing of Form 990 and the Unified Registration Statement (URS) required by most states. (An introduction to the URS is available on-line at www.nonprofits.org/library/gov/URS.) The project is developing both the front end—the error-detecting software that nonprofits and their tax preparers will use for filing (available at no cost from NCCS)—and the back-end system for smoothly processing payments, verifying the authenticity of filings, and transferring data to the eleven state charity offices.

The project is intended to lower the cost of collection and use of data for the state charity offices and improve the quality of Form 990 filings. It will also serve as a model for the national implementation of electronic filing now planned by the IRS. PRI, the IRS, and state charity officials currently spend millions of dollars each year to have information from Form 990 entered into databases. Not only is there duplication of effort, but the process of data entry introduces the potential for new errors. If all returns were electronically filed, there would be no need for any data entry.

The quality of the data on Form 990 is an ongoing concern. PRI estimates that approximately 80 percent of the returns are completed using tax preparation software. The vast majority of this software is bundled with general-purpose professional tax preparation software. Typically, an organization's auditors may charge several hundred dollars in addition to audit costs to complete the Form 990 once the audit has been completed. While current software appears to eliminate most arithmetic errors, sloppy returns are still a problem. For example, program services descriptions may be incomplete, most expenses may be attached on a schedule rather than being matched to the line numbers identified on the form, or board member titles are misspelled. The new NCCS software cannot prevent these mistakes altogether, but it can warn users about problem areas. The "tip" and "IRS Instruction" windows available to the user should also help improve the quality of the information. Finally, by offering an easy-to-use package for free, the NCCS hopes that the organizations that complete their returns on a typewriter or by hand will switch to the NCCS software, thus providing a return that has already been checked for errors.

The largest challenge for the project is the marketing challenge, not the technical one. The financial incentive of an early refund has propelled electronic filing of individual tax returns, but there is no comparable incentive for nonprofits to file electronically at this time. NCCS hopes that charities will respond to the availability of a free and easy-to-use system, but will be trying to reach both nonprofit organizations and their accountants to ensure that they are aware of the system. NCCS also expects that its current development work will stimulate software companies to add electronic filing for Form 990 to their tax preparation packages and perhaps improved error detection systems as well.

Nonprofit Internet data transmission standards. One of the major hurdles facing electronic filing efforts is the challenge of finding a common language that the variety of different tax preparation packages can use for transmitting data to regulatory database systems. Similar challenges are faced in the for-profit sector for transmitting not only tax data but also financial and business data generally. One solution that has strong backing from major software companies (especially Microsoft) is Extensible Markup Language, commonly known as XML. Closely related to HTML, the current language of the Web, XML standards are being developed in numerous areas of science and commerce as a means for transmitting data over the Web. All of these standards are open standards that anyone is free to use. One of the standards being developed is for business reporting (called eXtensible Business Reporting Language, or XBRL), which seems most relevant for the Form 990.

NCCS has joined the XBRL coalition, a group focused on developing a range of business reporting languages for use in transmitting financial statements, regulatory filings, and tax filing on the Web. In early 2001, NCCS developed XBRL for 990s, a system that it hopes can be used for electronic filing, both in its system and by any commercial tax preparation software. NCCS is also working with Micro Information Products, a major nonprofit accounting software company and a member of the XBRL coalition, to develop the XBRL Nonprofit Taxonomy, which will permit accounting systems to transmit standard nonprofit financial statements to tax preparation software, spreadsheets, and other applications. Simultaneously, the IRS is exploring the possibility of using XBRL or some other type of XML for its electronic filing systems.

Unified Chart of Accounts. The use of a standard chart of accounts that is electronically linked to the various reports required of nonprofits can also be a tool for improving the quality of nonprofit reporting. NCCS has helped develop the Unified Chart of Accounts (UCOA), a list of accounts that is cross-referenced to the various reporting requirements for nonprofits. UCOA provides a standard for nonprofit accounting and reporting systems, so that software developers and suppliers can create products that facilitate the preparation of reports usually required of nonprofits—for example, Form 990, registration and filing for state charity offices, reporting on grants for foundations and government, and financial reports for management and board use.

UCOA does not require that nonprofits change their accounting systems. Rather, the charts of accounts currently in use by organizations can be cross-walked electronically to UCOA. As the various accounts within UCOA are linked to the various reports required of nonprofits, accounting software can be used to generate the required reports using the standard account definitions. This approach was part of a pilot project in Tennessee to develop a chart of accounts that linked Form 990, generally accepted accounting principles, and the state's uniform government grant reporting requirements. It was further developed by the California Quality Reporting Task Force, sponsored by the California Association of Nonprofits and the California Society of Certified Public Accountants, and by CompassPoint, a nonprofit management support organization in San Francisco. The development of UCOA was a major component of the book *Unified Financial Reporting for Not-for-Profit Organizations* (Sumariwalla and Levis, 2000).

UCOA offers standard categories for tracking revenues, expenses, assets, and liabilities within accounting systems so that reports and forms, including Form 990, can be completed easily. For example, many organizations do not distinguish between the costs of holding a special event and other fundraising costs, while the Form 990 does. An organization that uses the UCOA will have already categorized its expenses so that special event expenses can be taken directly from its financial statements. In contrast, another organization attempting to complete its Form 990 may have to spend substantial time reviewing hundreds of expenses incurred over the course of a year in order to identify special event expenses. NCCS is working to promote this system, which promises to improve the consistency and accuracy of financial reports while easing the reporting burden for individual organizations.

State nonprofit database system. NCCS has created an easy-to-use database management system that incorporates the NCCS Form 990 data and provides numerous standardized reports, as well as tools for routine organization activities. The system is currently in use in a number of state affiliates of the National Council of Nonprofit Associations, primarily statewide associations of nonprofit organizations with no more than a handful of staff. It allows them to access and use the Form 990 data and provides basic systems for managing membership dues, events, and contacts. NCCS has recently expanded the system to meet the needs of state charity offices, state arts agencies, and a regional association of grant makers.

IRS-NASCO Activities. NCCS works closely with the IRS and NASCO to strengthen Form 990 as a source for useful and reliable information on nonprofit organizations. Unlike other IRS forms, Form 990 is explicitly intended to meet state as well as federal government needs. Thus, state charity officials play a key role in recommending improvements in the form. In order to support this role, NCCS hosts a two-part annual meeting with IRS and NASCO officials. One part is a closed meeting for IRS and NASCO officials only; the second part brings in representatives from the nonprofit sector, including staff from major umbrella organizations, IS, and the nonprofit accounting community. Typically, a set of recommendations for changes to Form 990 and its instructions is presented and discussed. The goal has been to find a way to add useful detail to Form 990 and clarifying instructions, but without adding substantially to the reporting burden. What is striking is the extent to which all parties at the table are able to discuss recommendations in a constructive and positive manner despite the major differences in interests and perspectives.

In the past year, NCCS has begun to take on an additional role with state charity offices. Over the years, NCCS has developed a good deal of expertise in working with Form 990 data and, more generally, with data on nonprofit organizations. Also, in work with the NCNA and the Unified Database of Arts Organizations, NCCS has learned a great deal about how to build a system for making data available in user-friendly format to nontechnical users. In 2000, it assisted the Charitable Trust Division of the State of Illinois in implementing a new database system for managing its registration process that also incorporated all of its Form 990 data.

Subsector collaboration. The organizational community of most nonprofit organizations is not "the nonprofit sector." Instead, it is the world of other organizations in the same field or subsector. A California opera company, for example, probably has a lot more in common with an opera company in Massachusetts than it has in common with a California nonprofit child care provider. This is one of the enduring challenges faced by IS and NCNA as they seek to represent the sector as a whole.

While virtually all nonprofit organizations collect basic financial data, the meaning of the data varies by subsector. For example, museums and housing organizations depend on facilities and real property and need financial reserves for facility maintenance, while foster care programs with leased office space do not. When measuring nonfinancial outcomes or performance indicators, the problem is even more acute. Number of persons served, for some organizations, captures a one-time interaction (attendance at a play), while for others, it may capture an intensive (and expensive) long-term commitment. Simplistic comparisons of cost per person are meaningless.

Some subsectors already have strong data collection systems. Where the nonprofit organizations tend to be large, strong nonprofit membership associations, the locus of most subsector data collection efforts, are often found. Thus, hospitals and higher education institutions have the strongest data collection systems in the nonprofit sector, while there is virtually no information beyond Form 990 on hundreds of thousands of small human service and community-based organizations. (The 350,000 religious congregations—organizations exempt from Form 990 filing—present an even greater challenge.) Although NCCS does not have the resources to address the data collection and accountability needs of all nonprofit subsectors, it has begun to develop some models for successful collaborations, especially in the arts.

The Unified Database of Arts Organizations is a joint project of the National Endowment for the Arts, the National Assembly of State Arts Agencies, and NCCS. The goal is to build a comprehensive database on arts organizations by merging IRS data, the extensive mailing and grantee listings of state arts agencies and the National Endowment for the Arts, along with data from arts service organizations and others. This database is available to researchers, funders, and policymakers and can be used for analysis or as a sampling frame. A new project with OPERA America,

Dance/USA, the American Symphony Orchestra League, the Association of Performing Arts Presenters, and the Theatre Communications group (funded by the Pew Charitable Trusts) will lead to the development of a uniform data collection system spanning the professional performing arts. This system will include not only detailed financial and operational data, but also will seek to measure the contribution of the performing arts in the lives of communities and individuals in ten cities.

Dissemination of data. The distribution of data to scholars and applied researchers working in umbrella organizations, foundations, and regulatory organizations is central to the NCCS mission. Having others use the data is an end in itself and is a key mechanism for testing and improving the quality of data. Knowledgeable reporters, practitioners, and regulators have also provided valuable insights on the uses and limitations of the NCCS data for accountability purposes.

Outcome and performance measurement. In both for-profit and nonprofit management circles, there has been an upsurge of interest in developing standardized performance indicators that move beyond the traditional focus on financial measurement to capture organizations' performance and prospects better. In the world of business management consulting, one sees a renewed emphasis on the value of measuring customer satisfaction and balanced scorecards that combine traditional financial measures with measures of internal process, customer satisfaction and perceptions, and the future potential of the organization (its learning and growth). In the nonprofit (and governmental) sector, the focus has been on outcome or performance measurement. (See Chapter Three of this volume.)

Performance measurement is not without its critics (see Frederickson, 2001). When dealing with complex social or psychological problems in the human services (providing mentoring services in a low-income, high-crime community, for example), it is difficult, if not impossible, to measure the impact of one small program. The cost of accurate and timely measurement can also be quite high. However, on the whole, this focus on performance measurement is a positive development for the sector.

The day-to-day activities of many nonprofit organizations are quite similar and, arguably, identical to the activities of their for-profit counterparts in the same subsectors or industries. For some, efficient and effective delivery of routine services or activities is paramount, and performance measurement tools used in business are readily translated to the nonprofit organizations. A focus on a range of performance measures, including innovation and experimentation, in recent literature on performance measurement moves in concept at least beyond the oversimplified measures that lead to a focus on, for example, short-term profits at the expense of long-term health.

Used wisely, performance measures serve as the basis for well-informed dialogue in the boardroom, among staff, and in policy debates about nonprofit activities and both their short- and long-term effects. The measures provide a language and a metric to ground the often-difficult debates about allocations of scarce resources for programs within an organization or for policymakers weighing the costs and benefits of supporting the nonprofit sector.

One approach to measurement is real time—that is, obtained during the ordinary course of providing services. A well-designed system that takes advantage of computer database technology, once put in place, should be relatively inexpensive to maintain. Staff members provide the information for the system as part of their regular routines, and managers can readily monitor and summarize performance measures. Often, the focus may be on the evaluation of the process rather than the outcome of the program, unless follow-up after completion of the service is included.

At the other end of the spectrum is periodic program evaluation, often conducted by outside evaluators, and popular among government agencies and large private foundations. While real-time performance measurement systems tend to produce quantifiable statistics, program evaluation tends toward more subjective assessments (Middleton, 1987).

NCCS is working to improve the information available in this area, for example, using and strengthening information found on Form 990 that deals with program service accomplishments. As a first step, NCCS has developed a system for classifying programs, services, and activities of nonprofits. Form 990 instructions also call for organizations to specify their program accomplishments, a concept closely allied with outcomes. While reporting of these accomplishments appears to be inadequate now, the increasing visibility of the form and its use by potential donors and funders will lead to improved data. NCCS will be using the available data for research and has also recommended expansion of this section to the IRS. Then organizations will clearly understand that quantifiable accomplishments are to be included in this section to the maximum extent possible. Finally, the Desktop 990 software developed for the electronic filing project includes separate fields for identifying accomplishments or outcomes.

In addition, NCCS has several projects that focus on identifying other sources of outcome data and on working to strengthen the capacity of nonprofit organizations to collect these data. One component of its work with a partnership of five performing arts umbrella associations entails the development of a set of audience, subscriber, and community household survey instruments that will be tested in ten pilot cities and are intended to measure the contribution that the performing arts make to individuals and to communities. NCCS expects to continue and expand this area of work in the future. It is also writing guidance to be used by community-based organizations funded by the Centers for Disease Control that are delivering HIV-AIDS prevention services, which are beginning to track the outcomes of their work.

Acccountable to whom?

Information is no tool for accountability unless there are people who will use it. This is an especially important matter for any discussion of accountability in the nonprofit sector since nonprofit organizations lack owners or shareholders who have vested interests in holding managers accountable. Lacking owners or shareholders, who really cares about the nonprofit sector? Who cares enough to hold the sector accountable? To some extent, the answer varies by type of organization.

A small number of federal and state regulators, members of the press, and scholars monitor or write about nonprofit accountability issues and tend to focus on larger organizations. Larger foundations or government funders require grantees to account for the use of their program funds. NCCS analysis of Form 990 data shows that approximately 32 percent of organizations with more than $100,000 in gross receipts reported government grants in 1998; in contrast, the number of organizations receiving major grants that invite foundation oversight is small.

Other candidates include large individual donors; people who live in neighborhoods near nonprofit organizations (the monitoring of group homes by neighbors is one example that has fueled controversy); a founder of an organization (which perhaps even bears the last name of the founder); the people in a community who have come to depend on an organization (community center, hospital, or summer recreation program) or are members of the parent-teacher association, community pool, or religious congregation; the students and faculty of a nonprofit university community; the families that have entrusted the care of a disabled or ill relative to a nursing home, group home, or hospice; the long-time volunteer or employee at the soup kitchen or theater; and the union representing workers at large hospitals and universities.

Most important in this web of accountability should be the board of directors. In the standard model of board governance (nonprofit or for-profit), the board has two major roles: (1) setting major policies and mapping strategy and (2) monitoring the performance of organization's chief executive officer. Better, more standardized data will help boards fulfill these responsibilities.

The emergence of a sector information system

Those who want to assess the accountability of charities have varied information and data needs. Some care about the specific effects of a program on individuals or neighborhoods (neighbors of a group home, families of a patient) and others about the fairness of compensation (unions); others care about overall program and organizational effectiveness or efficiency (the board or members of community association), or about excess benefits and private inurement (state and federal regulators). There are many others as well.

A sector information system integrating information collected by NCCS, PRI, the Foundation Center, IS, the National Center for Nonprofit Boards, state charity offices, the IRS, private foundations, subsector umbrella associations, researchers, program evaluators, and others seems the ideal vehicle for meeting the broad needs of these groups. In some respects, such an informal system may be emerging as various organizations place data and information on the Web. However, despite major advances by PRI and others, available information falls far short of what is possible or what is needed for potential users to have the information they need to make informed decisions. Richer data and information are not substitutes for sound judgment, but they should provide the basis for better decision making by boards, funders, and others and ultimately lead to a more effective, efficient, and successful nonprofit sector.

In an idealized image of nonprofit board process, well-informed citizen board members come together to deliberate democratically about strategy and policy. Boards and staff of many organizations must make decisions about program expansion, funding opportunities to pursue, staff compensation levels, and a myriad of other issues. These decisions ought to be informed by sound information. But in reality, many volunteer board members lead busy lives and have little time for their board duties. The cost of finding, organizing, and presenting the full range of information that would be required for optimal board decision making is high. Staff are equally busy and also face temptations to present only the information that supports their interests and viewpoints. Lacking adequate information, board members are more likely to defer to the executive director, to be influenced by outspoken and opinionated board members, and to rely on limited or idiosyncratic experience or opinions. A sector information system that provided comprehensive, well-organized, and free (or perhaps low-cost) information could improve the dynamics of board decision making. The goal is not to eliminate the deference to the executive director altogether or eliminate the role of a board member's experience and personal judgment; it is, however, to provide a rich information environment without which accountability can too easily become an empty concept.

More broadly, NCCS is working to help provide a rich information environment that will support the difficult tasks and decisions faced by those who are accountable for the nonprofit sector. We believe that in the long term, this will lead to a stronger and more effective sector.

References

"A Baltimore Case Explores Do's and Don'ts as Unions Take to the Internet." *Wall Street Journal*, Apr. 17, 2001, p. 1.

Brilliant, E. L. *Private Charity and Public Inquiry: A History of the Filer and Peterson Commissions.* Bloomington, Ind.: Indiana University Press, 2000.

Cordes, J. J., Pollak, T. H., and Wilson, S. "Fundraising and Administrative Costs in the Nonprofit Sector." Paper presented at the Association for Research on Nonprofit Organizations and Voluntary Action, Washington, D.C., November, 1999.

Emerson, J. "Grantee-Grantor Relations: Mutual Accountability and the Wisdom of Frank Capra." *Foundation News and Commentary*, 2001, *42*, 42–46.

Frederickson, H. G. "Lessons Learned: First There's Theory. Then, There's Practice." *Foundation News and Commentary*, 2001, *42*, 37–41.

Froelich, K., and Knoepfle, T. "Internal Revenue Service 990 Data: Fact or Fiction?" *Nonprofit and Voluntary Sector Quarterly*, 1996, *25*, 40–52.

Froelich, K. A., Knoepfle, T. W., and Pollak, T. H. "Financial Measures in Nonprofit Organization Research: Comparing IRS 990 Return and Audited Financial Statement Data." *Nonprofit and Voluntary Sector Quarterly*, 2000, *29*, 232–254.

Gaul, G. M., and Borowski, N. A. "Warehouses of Wealth: The Tax-Free Economy." *Philadelphia Inquirer*, Apr. 18–23, 1993, pp. 1, 11, 12, 27.

Greenlee, J. S., and Gordon, T. "The Impact of Professional Solicitors on Fund-Raising in Charitable Organizations." *Nonprofit and Voluntary Sector Quarterly*, 1998, *27*, 277–299.

Hall, P. D. "A Historical Overview of the Private Nonprofit Sector." In W. W. Powell (ed.), *The Nonprofit Sector: A Research Handbook.* New Haven, Conn.: Yale University Press, 1987.

Hammack, D. C. "Accountability and Nonprofit Organizations: A Historical Perspective." *Nonprofit Management and Leadership*, 1995, *6*, 137–139.
Haycock, N. *The Nonprofit Sector in New York City*. New York: Nonprofit Coordinating Committee of New York, 1992.
Herzlinger, R. "Can Public Trust in Nonprofits and Governments Be Restored?" *Harvard Business Review*, Mar.–Apr. 1996, 97–107.
Kanter, R. M., and Summers, D. V. "Doing Well While Doing Good: Dilemmas of Performance Measurement in Nonprofit Organizations and the Need for a Multiple-Constituency Approach." In W. W. Powell (ed.), *The Nonprofit Sector: A Research Handbook*. New Haven, Conn.: Yale University Press, 1987.
McLean, Charles, and L. M. Lampkin. "Now That We Have the Data, Can We Use Them? Assessing the Quality of IRS Form 990 Data." Paper presented at the Association for Research on Nonprofit Organizations and Voluntary Action, Washington, DC, November, 1999.
Middleton, M. "Nonprofit Boards of Directors: Beyond the Governance Function." In W. W. Powell (ed.), *The Nonprofit Sector: A Research Handbook*. New Haven, Conn.: Yale University Press, 1987.
Pollak, T., and Pettit, K. S. "The Finances of Operating Public Charities, 1989–1995." Working paper, Urban Institute, 1997.
Stevenson, D., Pollak, T., and Lampkin, L. *The State Nonprofit Almanac 1997*. Washington, D.C.: Urban Institute Press, 1997.
Sumariwalla, R., and Levis, B. *Unified Financial Reporting for Not-for-Profit Organizations: A Comprehensive Guide to Unifying GAAP, IRS Form 990, and Other Financial Reports Using a Unified Chart of Accounts*. San Francisco: Jossey-Bass, 2000.

THOMAS H. POLLAK *is Assistant Director of the National Center for Charitable Statistics, a program of the Center on Nonprofits and Philanthropy at the Urban Institute in Washington, D.C.*

LINDA M. LAMPKIN *is Program Director of the National Center for Charitable Statistics (NCCS), a program of the Center on Nonprofits and Philanthropy at the Urban Institute in Washington, D.C.*

State charity regulation is an important form of oversight for nonprofit activities. There are initiatives underway to improve consistency among the states and adapt policies to the growing practice of seeking donations online.

6

On accountability: A state charity official's prospective

Daniel Moore

ACCOUNTABILITY IS one of the most critical issues facing the social sector in the United States today. On May 24, 2000, for example, six leading national organizations—the Council on Foundations, Council of Better Business Bureaus, INDEPENDENT SECTOR, National Charities Information Bureau, National Center for Nonprofit Boards, National Council of Nonprofit Associations, and United Way of America—convened the symposium Accountability in the Sector. *Accountability*, however, is a slippery term that means different things to different people.

Stated broadly, in discussions about nonprofits, *accountability* usually refers to preserving the public's trust in a sector that exists solely to serve the public's interest. For many regulators of charitable activities, accountability means providing evidence that an organization is fulfilling the fiduciary duties that come with the stewardship responsibilities implicit in the charitable trust

Note: The views in this chapter are those of the author and not the official views of the New Mexico attorney general or the National Association of State Charity Officials.

impressed on the assets given to further the nonprofit organization's mission. Others argue that if donors continue to make voluntary contributions to a charitable organization, then the organization has passed "a market test," and nothing more is required.

Along this continuum is the struggle to define with more precision the meaning of *accountability* in the social sector. There continues to exist a need for people of goodwill who have the best interests of the sector in mind to come together to engage in dialogue and attempt to forge a working consensus on accountability.

The critical role of the nonprofit sector in democratic society

It is important for everyone, but perhaps especially for government officials, to acknowledge the critical role that the social sector plays in protecting, preserving, and advancing the democratic character of our society. People coming together to address community needs has been an enduring quality of the American character. Enshrined in our Constitution's First Amendment, we exercise our rights to associate freely, speak freely, and petition the government through these voluntary institutions. In many ways, service on nonprofit boards acts as an incubator for future business and government leaders. Through voluntary action, we renew our sense of community and give meaning to our lives.

Many observers comment that the role of the social sector will only become greater in this century. One such leading voice, Peter F. Drucker, comments:

> The 21st century will be the century of the social sector organization. The more economy, money and information become global, the more community will matter. And only the social sector nonprofit organization performs in the community, exploits its opportunities, mobilizes its local resources, solves its problems. The leadership, competence, and management of the social sector nonprofit organization will largely determine the

values, the vision, the cohesion, and the performance of the 21st century society [Drucker Foundation 1999, p. 1].

The need to protect, preserve, and strengthen the social sector for service to society will require leadership by the sector, government, and accountability advocates. Defining a common agenda is needed in order to communicate a message to the public effectively and marshal the resources necessary to strengthen the sector to create a better world.

Common ground and battleground: Government and nonprofits

The nature of the government and social sector relationship is complex. Sometimes cooperative, sometimes combative, sometimes collaborative, the government-nonprofit relationship is vital to the functioning of democracy. I focus more narrowly though on the topic of government oversight to ensure that social sector organizations are legitimate and accountable. (For important insights on this topic, see Ormstedt, 1994; Knowles, 1996.)

Because charitable organizations are dedicated to a public purpose, state charity officials have an important role in overseeing and enforcing the charitable purposes of these otherwise private institutions. The legal basis for this authority lies in the common law tradition, which is often supplemented by specific statutory authority. It is often the state attorney general, as the legal representative of the community, who is empowered to ensure that charitable gifts made for a public purpose are properly applied. Laws in certain states have delegated certain responsibilities to the office of the secretary of state and other non–attorney general's offices for oversight of charitable solicitations and other charitable activities.

Laws vary by state, but at its essence, the mission of state charity officials is fairly straightforward. State charity officials are charged by law to (1) protect donors against deceptive solicitations,

(2) represent the interests of the charitable beneficiaries to ensure that the donor's intent is complied with, and (3) ensure that the trustees fulfill their stewardship responsibilities for the charitable assets under their care.

One important element in the ways state charity officials attempt to accomplish this important mission is a regulatory system that requires registration and financial reporting from charitable organizations and their paid fundraisers. State charity officials have frequent contact with donors to charitable causes who are inquiring about the charitable solicitations they have received. These officials respond to complaints about a charity or about its fundraiser, initiate investigations of alleged wrongdoing, and take appropriate enforcement actions. State charity officials conduct public outreach campaigns to deter fraud and to promote wise giving. Other public outreach campaigns attempt to strengthen the governing capabilities of nonprofit boards.

By and large, nonprofit leaders agree with and support the mission of state charity officials as an essential element of their accountability responsibilities to the public. The common ground becomes more of a battleground when the focus shifts from the mission to the methods of accomplishing the mission.

Critics take issue with the current regulatory system, especially for charitable organizations that are required to register and report in multiple states. Critics also take issue with some of the public outreach efforts, especially the emphasis on fundraising expenses. Some criticize elected officials for grandstanding and for what they see as politically motivated enforcement actions.

The current state-by-state, paper-based filing system requires significant investments of money and staff time to manage. A recent survey of state charity officials shows that nearly two-thirds of the regulators' time is spent on registration and unregistered solicitation activities (Sandoe-Connor, 2000). Only 16 percent of their time is spent on addressing nonprofit abuses, such as the misappropriation of funds and breaches of duty by the governing board. The goal of creating a more effective oversight system will demand greater efficiencies in managing the registration process and a shift of resources toward more analysis of the information that nonprofit organizations file and more enforcement addressing nonprofit abuses.

The Internet: The new frontier

One of the most important and powerful forces transforming society in the 1990s has been the digital revolution. The Internet has transformed and continues to transform how we buy and sell stocks, airline tickets, music, and just about everything else. The Internet moves at a speed that has far exceeded the ability of government and our system of laws to catch up. The resulting gap has left many pioneers of new forms of commerce in a limbo of uncertainty. This is particularly true for social sector nonprofit organizations (Nooney 2000; Livingston, 2001).

All observers agree that the Internet has lowered the barriers for smaller organizations to reach a national and even international audience. I know this from firsthand experience. As the creator of the National Association of State Charity Officials (NASCO) Web site (www.nasconet.org), I know that for a small investment, any organization can have a presence on the World Wide Web. Unfortunately, the Internet has also lowered the barriers for charitable solicitation fraud, a subject that should concern all who seek to protect this important new space for philanthropy, dubbed e-philanthropy, to grow and flourish.

The Internet, however, has not substantially altered the nature of the donor-organization relationship. The organization still makes a promise to the donor to accomplish a particular public good. The donor still must have some confidence and trust that the organization will fulfill its promise.

The Internet, however, has made it more efficient for the organization to cultivate and build this vital relationship. E-mail updates sent to donors to inform and build relationships offer the promise that organizations may be more accountable to their donors through more frequent and targeted communication. A Web site that educates and informs donors about the good works of an organization creates a new tool to build community between donors, actual and prospective, and the organization.

The Internet has not changed the character of the human heart either. Deceptive charitable solicitations are a problem in the online as much as in the real world. In either setting, fraud has a corrosive effect on the public's trust and confidence in charitable activities. The Internet creates a new medium for charitable solicitation fraud. Leaders in the social sector and in government and accountability advocates must develop effective strategies to protect this space for philanthropic activity.

Organizations like the Association of Fundraising Professionals and the ePhilanthropy Foundation are attempting to issue guidelines and set ethical standards for online activities. These positive and proactive steps demonstrate thoughtful leadership by the sector (Warwick, Hart, and Allen, 2001).

The Charleston Principles: Toward regulation of e-philanthropy

Beginning in the summer of 1999, state charity officials began serious discussion and study of whether and how current laws governing charitable solicitations apply to the Internet. The annual NASCO conference, held in Charleston, South Carolina, that year expanded the dialogue to include nonprofit leaders.

As a state charity official, I continue to be grateful for the generous and cooperative spirit of social sector leaders like Putnam Barber, Buzz Schmidt, Nick Allen, Ian Hughes, and others too numerous to mention who have engaged state charity officials in thoughtful discussions of the emerging e-philanthropy.

As a result of this meeting and subsequent internal discussion, NASCO leaders produced "The Charleston Principles: Guidelines on Charitable Solicitations Using the Internet." To obtain a copy of the Charleston Principles, visit the NASCO Web site at www.NASCOnet.org. The principal authors of the Charleston Principles are Jeff Even, assistant attorney general in the Washington State attorney general's office; Nikki Trella, legal officer in the Maryland secretary of state's office; and me.

In August 2000, NASCO released a draft of the Charleston Principles on its Web site and provided a mechanism to receive comments on-line about the principles. At its annual meeting in San Diego in October 2000 and at numerous conferences and meetings around the country, NASCO leaders engaged nonprofit leaders in dialogue about the principles. On March 14, 2001, the NASCO governing board adopted the principles and distributed them to its members as a guide to assist state charity offices in establishing state-specific policy governing Internet charitable solicitations.

When these issues first began to be discussed, many state charity officials took the position that "if I can see your Web site with its charitable solicitation, then you must register in my state." This view had tremendous ramifications. By most state laws, a solicitation is deemed to have occurred whether a donation is actually given by a donor. It is in the asking, and not in the receiving, that a solicitation has occurred. By this logic, every charity with a Web site would be required to register in every state that requires charitable solicitation registration.

This logic, though, had a paradoxical result. The medium that lowered the barriers to a national audience would be closed to all but the big groups. State charity offices struggling with thousands and tens of thousands of registrations and annual reports could be flooded with thousands and thousands of new registrations. The prospect was a nightmare for charities and for regulators. Worse yet, this policy, if followed and enforced, was a ticket straight to some federal court to test the legal basis of that position by the state that was sued first.

The Charleston Principles arose from a process of deliberate study and discussion among regulators and between state charity officials and nonprofit leaders. With the real possibility that litigation was looming large, an analysis of court decisions on personal jurisdiction and the Internet was necessary to construct a defensible legal position for the states and to preserve any role for state oversight of charitable solicitations on the Internet (Liazos, 2000).

It is important to understand the limitations of the Charleston Principles in order to be clear what they are and what they are not. They are not a model law or a directive from the NASCO board to its members. A voluntary association of members representing sovereign states has no such authority. The Charleston Principles are a guide to assist states in crafting their own policy consistent with their own laws. The Charleston Principles are also a signal to the nonprofit community about how states may act on this important matter. They embody a process of inclusion and consultation in which nonprofit leaders had a seat at the table from the earliest opportunity.

The key principles are these:

Although existing state laws govern charitable solicitations on the Internet, in many instances the use of the Internet raises new questions that state charity officials must answer in order to effectively carry out their statutory missions.

State charity officials should require registration of those over whom their state courts could constitutionally assert personal jurisdiction to enforce a registration requirement.

Deceptive charitable solicitations and fraud can, should, and will be prosecuted by any state when its citizens are victims of such fraud.

The "if we can see it" test for chaitable solicitations was challenged; in its place, the Charleston Principles propose a "repeated, ongoing, or substantial contribution" test. This means that an out-of-state charity whose only contact with a state is over the Internet should be required to register in that state only if the charity actually receives contributions from residents of that state on a repeated, ongoing, or substantial basis. Specific guidance from the states is needed to give definition to this new standard.

An interesting dialogue began within the NASCO community of charity regulators. Prosecutors wanted a vaguer standard so that enforcement actions could be brought without limitations of a specific standard articulated in some guidelines. Administrators of charitable registration offices needed brighter lines that could be easily communicated to charities that wanted to know the rules in order to comply with them. This conversation took place all within the context of representatives of sovereign states insisting on their state's right to set their state's own policy. The glue that kept the discussion going was the skillful leadership of the NASCO board and the genuine dedication of NASCO members to public service and law enforcement.

Time will tell whether the Charleston Principles will form the basis of a consensus on how states will individually apply their laws. It is clear from the dialogue that consistency and uniformity are highly valued by the sector, especially in the on-line world.

The dot.com collapse in e-philanthropy in late 2000 and 2001 has removed much of the sense of urgency for a solution. The rest of the story of the Charleston Principles is yet to be told.

It is clear that the Internet is changing philanthropy and has a great potential to bring people together, create community, and perhaps raise money for philanthropic causes. It is also clear that the rise of e-philanthropy has presented a new and a compelling challenge to the current state-by-state paper registration system for charitable oversight. This system is incompatible with a strategy for effective government oversight of charitable activities in the twenty-first century.

More effective government oversight of charitable activities

How to create more effective government oversight of charitable activities is an important part of the accountability discussion. One thing is certain: the growth of the sector in terms of numbers has outpaced government's response.

Ineffective government oversight places unnecessary burdens on charitable organizations where "good" organizations struggle to comply with a maze of rules and regulations and "bad" groups game a system that is overburdened and underfunded. Ineffective government oversight allocates resources in ways that do not provide the public with the highest value for necessary government services. And oversight of charitable activities is a necessary government service. An allocation of resources that expends nearly two-thirds of its assets on a registration system and less than one-fifth of its time and energy on addressing nonprofit abuses is by definition ineffective. Finally, and most important, ineffective government oversight provides the public with false confidence that someone is minding the store. The media's focus on charity scandal and abuse is unlikely to change. Public confidence in an effective government response to combat charity abuses must be maintained. If that effort fails, there will be growing public distrust and loss of confidence in social sector organizations as a whole. It is potentially a lose-lose-lose proposition.

A new federal agency for nonprofits

The current model of state-by-state registration of charitable solicitation activities has many critics. Some argue that the inefficiencies of the current system and the importance of preserving public confidence in charitable activities require a new, and perhaps a federal, solution. These critics argue that an agency for charitable activities similar in scope to the Securities and Exchange Commission (SEC) needs to be created or empowered to oversee these activities. This idea is not a new one. It was one of the recommendations of the Commission on Private Philanthropy and Public Needs (also known, after its chair, as the Filer Commission) in the mid-seventies that was never acted on (Brilliant, 2000, pp. 144–147; Fishman and Schwarz, 1999; Fleishman, 1999; Herzlinger, 1996).

Herzlinger (1996) argues that an SEC model of regulation would promote effective government oversight of charitable organization. This kind of regulatory system would focus on disclosure, analysis, dissemination of performance information, and sanctions against organizations that do not comply with those requirements. Herzlinger views public disclosure of nonfinancial quantitative information as necessary to ensure that nonprofit organizations are fulfilling their missions.

Fleishman (1999) argues that there are two distinct and quite different problems that must be resolved in order to solve the accountability-enforcement crisis that he concludes threatens the public's trust in the nonprofit sector. The first problem is posed by the fake charities and unscrupulous groups and individuals who defraud the public in the name of charity. The second is the "unwise, injudicious, or careless—but not illegal—patterns of action by bona fide not-for-profit organizations" (p. 186).

Fleishman poses three alternative solutions: (1) a not-for-profit sector strategy, (2) a joint not-for-profit sector–governmental strategy, and (3) a new federal agency for policing and defending the not-for-profit sector.

The not-for-profit sector strategy calls on the sector to police itself through a new group that would act much like a professional ethics enforcement body to investigate complaints and turn bad actors over to the authorities for appropriate punishment. This self-policing body would set standards appropriate to the diversity of the sector that go beyond the minimum legal requirements. Finally, this group would be an advocate for effective government oversight and would take responsibility for recommending desirable changes in state and federal law to promote accountability.

The joint not-for-profit sector–government strategy calls for private philanthropy to support financially the work of NASCO to create a national clearinghouse of information on abuses by nonprofit organizations, investigate instances of such abuse, and work jointly with the appropriate state and federal authorities to bring bad actors to justice. Fleishman credits NASCO with efforts to streamline the multistate registration process through its Unified Registration Statement. While reforming the registration process is important, Fleishman points to where NASCO could be more effective in supporting enforcement activities.

The new federal agency is Fleishman's strategy of last resort, to be considered only if the other strategies have failed. A U.S.

charities regulatory commission that Fleishman suggests would be similar to the SEC model that Herzlinger offers, but Fleishman sees the new agency working closely with the Exempt Organizations Office of the Internal Revenue Service (IRS) and the Federal Trade Commission. Importantly, Fleishman argues against any federal preemption of state enforcement authority, as he views an effective state presence as necessary to any effective oversight strategy.

Forging more effective federal-state cooperation

Other critics of the current system point to restrictions in the current tax code that severely limit the potential partnerships between state charity officials and the IRS. These restrictions limit the effectiveness of the current federal-state regulatory system (Lyon, 1996).

The National Association of Attorneys General (NAAG) has passed numerous resolutions calling for reform legislation. In 1994, the NAAG resolution called for federal legislation that would

(a) relax provisions of Section 6103 of the Internal Revenue Code to permit the sharing of audit and examination information and records for Section 501(c)(3) and 501(c)(4) organizations with state agencies with jurisdiction over activities of those organizations;
(b) encourage cooperation between the IRS and state regulators by permitting immediate and ongoing feedback when a state agency makes a referral;
(c) establish regional task forces consisting of personnel from IRS' regional exempt organizations offices and state regulators from within that region to encourage the sharing of information, training, and participation in cooperative investigations among task force members.

These calls for reform have not gone unheard on Capitol Hill. For example, the 1993–1994 Pickle Hearing report included a recommendation by the House Subcommittee that "IRS study and make recommendations to the Committee on Way and Means on whether certain State officers, such as the attorney general and other officials charged with overseeing public charities, should be provided additional access to Federal tax information" [Lyon, 1996, p. §5.04[3] 5-28 to 5-29].

In January 2000, the U.S. Congress's Joint Committee on Taxation's *Study of Disclosure Provisions Relating to Tax-Exempt Organi-*

zations recommended changes to section 6103 of the Internal Revenue Code to provide more effective communication between the IRS and state charity officials. In the opinion of the joint committee, such changes would

(1) enhance the combined efforts of the Federal and State governments to protect the public by promoting the continued flow of information from State officials to the IRS;
(2) improve the ability of State officials to monitor compliance with non-tax State laws affecting tax-exempt organizations and to enforce and pursue correction of violations of such laws; and
(3) facilitate the participation of both the IRS and State officials in the resolution of cases involving significant charitable and fiduciary violations by making more complete information available in earlier phases of such cases to both State officials and the IRS" [U.S. Congress, 2000, pp. 104–105].

A new registration and reporting model

If we did not have the current state-by-state registration and reporting model for charitable solicitations, no one would create it as an effective means of promoting nonprofit accountability and government oversight of charitable activities.

Charitable organizations file Form 990 with the IRS, which processes the returns and stores them. It then key-punches many key fields in the return transaction file. An organization that solicits contributions on a national basis files the same paper return in thirty-nine states and the District of Columbia. In each of the state offices, the same return is processed and stored. Each state key-punches key fields—often the same fields. The cost and duplication of the system is no small matter. In an era before e-mail and the Internet, this duplication was arguably necessary. Today, it is hard to justify and defend.

The Internet, while raising challenges to the question of which organizations should register with which states, also offers a solution. Electronic filing with the IRS and the states would streamline the registration and reporting system, eliminating the duplication of efforts for charitable organizations and the IRS and state charity offices. The efficiencies in an e-file solution would create cost savings in the administration of the registration and reporting system, allowing a reallocation of resources to analysis and appropriate enforcement.

The pioneering work of Philanthropic Research, Inc. (PRI), the creator and operator of the GuideStar Web site, and its partners at the National Center for Charitable Statistics (NCCS) of the Urban Institute have taken giant steps toward a new model of disclosure (see Chapter Five in this issue). The project with the IRS to scan images of Form 990 and convert the images into files that can be easily displayed and viewed via the Internet has profound implications. In addition to the public disclosure value of the GuideStar Web site, PRI and NCCS are digitizing nearly the entire Form 990. In 2001, about three years of Form 990s were scanned, digitized, and posted online. Leaders in the sector in government and accountability advocates have not yet begun to mine these data and communicate their results. The project has enormous potential to reshape the accountability discussion.

A new registration model is needed to replace the current state-by-state, paper-based system. It is not yet evident what exactly this new model will look like, but some values that a successful new model should incorporate are becoming clear:

- *Keep it simple.* Charities want a simplified compliance system. Filing electronically in one place at one time, a charity using such a system could fulfill the reporting requirements for all states that require registration and for the IRS. Local governments could also have easy access to these records without adding new reporting requirements on the charities. Local governments could continue to enforce registration of door-to-door solicitations. Enforcement actions taken against false, misleading, or deceptive solicitations would remain a bona-fide activity for governments at the state and local level.
- *Serve multiple users of the data at the same time.* A central electronic document repository that included important compliance documents like the Articles of Incorporation, IRS Letter of Determination, IRS Form 1023, and three years of IRS Form 990, for

example, could satisfy state reporting requirements, IRS disclosure requirements, and due diligence requirements for private and public grant makers. Whether a state, federal, or private administrator maintains such a site is not as important as realizing the cost savings for the social sector and government by eliminating duplicative reporting.

- *Reduce compliance costs.* Wasting charitable assets is offensive to state charity officials, nonprofit leaders, and donors. The efficiencies of information technology can help bring about a more cost-effective system. Reducing compliance costs is a means for redirecting charitable assets to serve the needs of the charitable beneficiaries better. Reducing compliance costs for government creates the opportunity to shift resources from administrative functions into investigations and enforcement actions.
- *Promote accountability through appropriate transparency.* Although not all of the affairs of charitable organizations should be subject to public disclosure and scrutiny, the public is entitled to complete, timely, and accurate financial and program-related information about charities.

Creating a new registration and reporting system is not without substantial challenges. State laws governing charitable solicitations would need to be made uniform. This change cannot be accomplished without a sectorwide consensus formed in partnership with government charity regulators. One critical change would require a harmonizing of the disparate fees charged to the same organization by different states. This issue poses a serious challenge to the entire reform effort.

Conclusion

The challenges are not insurmountable but will require leadership, skill, and perhaps a little luck. Success will require a consensus among leaders in the social sector and government and accountability advocates to serve the best interest of the sector and the public it exists to serve. Reaching consensus requires meaningful dialogue, skilled leadership, and a desire to serve the public's interest. This important work has already begun.

References

Brilliant, E. L. *Private Charity and Public Inquiry: A History of the Filer and Peterson Commissions.* Bloomington: Indiana University Press, 2000.

Drucker Foundation. *Annual Report.* New York, N.Y.: Drucker Foundation, 1999.

Fishman, J. J., and Schwarz, S. eds. "Proposal for Reform: Federal Regulation of Charitable Solicitation." In *Nonprofit Organizations: Cases and Materials.* (2nd ed.) Westbury, N.Y.: Foundation Press, 1999.

Fleishman, J. L. "Public Trust in Not-for-Profit Organizations and the Need for Regulatory Reform." In C. T. Clotfelter and T. Ehrlich (eds.), *Philanthropy and the Nonprofit Sector in a Changing America.* Bloomington: Indiana University Press, 1999.

"Government regulation of fundraising: A struggle for efficacy" in *New Directions for Philanthropic Fundraising*, Number 3, Spring 1994, James M. Greenfield, editor and Terry M. Knowles "A Brief History of Charitable Regulation" in the New Hampshire Bar Journal, December 1996.

Herzlinger, R. "Can Public Trust in Nonprofits and Governments Be Restored?" *Harvard Business Review*, Mar.–Apr. 1996, 97–107.

Knowles, T. M., 1996. "A Brief History of Charitable Regulation." *New Hampshire Bar Journal*, Vol. 37, No. 4, 8–13, Dec. 1996.

Liazos, M. G. "Can States Impose Registration Requirements On Online Charitable Solicitors." *University of Chicago Law Review*, Vol. 67, 1379–1407, Fall 2000.

Livingston, C. E. "Tax-Exempt Organizations and the Internet: Tax and Other Legal Issues," *Exempt Organizations Tax Review*, 419–436, March, 2001. http://www.tax.org/tcom/international/eotr.htm

Lyon, J. B. 1996. "The Supervision of Charities in the United States by State Attorneys General (and Other State Agencies) and the Internal Revenue Service." Paper presented at New York University's Twenty-Fourth conference on Tax Planning for 501(c)(3) Organizations, New York, 1996.

Nooney, C. L. "Tax-Exempt Organizations and the Internet." *Exempt Organization Tax Review*, 2000, January, Vol. 27, No. 1, 33–48.

Ormstedt, D. "Government Regulation of Fundraising: A Struggle for Efficacy." In J. M. Greenfield (ed.) *Financial Practices for Effective Fundraising*, New Directions for Philanthropic Fundraising, no. 3. San Francisco: Jossey-Bass, 1994.

Sandoe-Connor, L. L. "Charity Fraud: Is the Current Regulatory System Holding the Nonprofit Sector Accountable?" Unpublished master's thesis, Pennsylvania State University, 2000.

U.S. Congress. Joint Committee on Taxation. *Study of Present-Law Taxpayer Confidentiality and Disclosure Provisions as Required by Section 3802 of the Inter-*

nal Revenue Service Restructuring and Reform Act of 1998, Vol. II: *Study of Disclosure Provisions Relating to Exempt Organizations.* Washington, D.C.: U.S. Government Printing Office, Jan. 28, 2000.

Warwick, M. Hart, T., and Allen, N. (eds.). *Fundraising on the Internet: The e-Philanthropy Foundation Organization's Guide to Success Online*. (2nd ed.) San Francisco: Jossey-Bass, 2001.

DANIEL MOORE *is the registrar of charitable organizations in New Mexico's attorney general's office and the chief charity regulator for the state. At the time of writing he was also president of the National Association of State Charity Officials.*

Accountability is essential to the viability of the nonprofit sector, but can disclosure obligations and government oversight impede charities' abilities to serve the public interest?

7

The nonprofit sector and accountability

Sara E. Melendéz

THE INDEPENDENT SECTOR—grant-making and nonprofit organizations—must earn the public trust every day in order to ensure donors of their trustworthiness and effectiveness. Donors do not contribute to organizations they do not trust and about which they do not feel confident. The sector organizations also depend on the trust of regulatory and oversight bodies to perform their roles effectively, provide guidance and advice, and help them comply with the law. When regulators and enforcement agencies perform their roles effectively, the related complications are kept to an appropriate level, and their efforts facilitate the work of the nonprofit organizations.

Whereas government is primarily accountable to voters and the corporate sector is accountable to shareholders, the nonprofit sector is accountable to donors, volunteers, clients, the media, and government. The public expects a higher level of accountability from the nonprofit sector both because of its tax treatment and because

Note: An earlier version of this chapter was delivered at the National Association of State Charities Officials conference in San Diego, October 2000.

it is seen as the "do-good" sector. Change the last sentence to: The rewards for meeting this higher expectation are that the public rates the sector organizations significantly higher on trustworthiness than government or business (INDEPENDENT SECTOR, 2001a, p. 2). Further, nearly 89 percent of households give an average of 3.2 percent of their income, or $1620 in 2001, to their congregations and favorite charities (INDEPENDENT SECTOR, 2001b, p. 3).

The leadership of the philanthropic and nonprofit sector understands how essential this public trust is to the viability of their organizations. Indeed, in sector discussions about accountability, openness, and disclosure, a common phrase used is "obedience to the unenforceable." This implies that the organizations of the sector must go beyond mere obedience to the laws and conduct their business with adherence to the espoused and implied values of the sector, such as private initiative for the public good, service to individuals and communities, and providing a voice for the voiceless. This is not an insignificant expectation, given the size, scope, and diversity of missions and methodologies of the sector.

America's independent sector is a diverse collection of more than 1 million charitable organizations. It is these groups that create, nurture, and sustain the values that frame American life and strengthen democracy. This sector employs more than 11 million individuals and an additional 5.7 million full-time equivalent employees who volunteer. The sector generates almost seven percent of national income and has revenues in excess of $660 billion annually (INDEPENDENT SECTOR ctor, 2001c, pp. 7–8).

The size and impact of the sector make it essential that the sector organizations be accountable for compliance with the law, prudent use of the donated funds, and adherence to the highest standards of practice and ethics. The issue of accountability seems to acquire major significance when the budget of a nonprofit organization is in the hundreds of millions of dollars and serves millions of individuals annually. A nonprofit organization with a budget of less than twenty-five thousand dollars—the majority of organizations—can make a mistake or even commit a crime and go unnoticed. But when an organization's budget is in the millions, the impact of its error or felony can be significant. It is not surprising, therefore, that the increasing attention to the issue of accountability and the increased coverage of the sector by the media are concurrent with the phenomenal growth in the number of grantmaking and nonprofit organizations and the growth of the assets of both grant makers and public charities.

What is included in reasonable accountability?

Accountability includes many factors, such as compliance with the law and reporting requirements, openness, ethical practices, adherence to quality standards, and demonstration of effectiveness and outcomes. Disclosure is an important part of accountability. The leadership and donors of the independent sector have a keen interest in ensuring that charities provide public disclosure of key information to help ensure that they operate strictly in the public interest and not for private benefit. They know that charities depend on public trust to raise money, secure volunteers, and carry out their missions and that disclosure and transparency are essential to maintaining that trust. They also understand the necessity of reasonable government oversight and review.

Charities must operate with a high degree of transparency to ensure the public trust essential to the performance of their social role. However, some would claim that the tax "subsidy" gives the public the right to require charities to give up any right to privacy. Charities, however, are fundamentally private entities and as such are entitled to a substantial zone of privacy with respect to their internal decision-making process. Moreover, confidentiality is essential to fair and efficient tax administration.

Charities' disclosure obligation derives not from their tax treatment but from their role in serving public interests. Many taxable entities receive exemptions for part of their income or tax benefits of comparable value. A 2000 report of the congressional Joint Committee on Taxation (JCT) recommended mandating increased reporting on charities' participation in the public policy process, while recognizing that tax benefits do not justify mandatory disclosure of return information by taxable entities and individuals. (U.S. Congress, 2000).The requirement should be no different for charities and other exempt entities.

The burden of additional disclosure with respect to public policy–related activities will create a chilling effect on charities' participation in the development of public policy, an effect that is not in the public interest. Voluntary organizations, funded by private contributions, were at the center of most of the policy innovations in the twentieth century and continue to be. Any policy, regulatory, or legislative action that inhibits citizen action is to be avoided, even as reasonable, appropriate policies are supported.

Disclosure obligations

The JCT report suggests that charities' public disclosure obligations derive principally from their favorable tax treatment—that is, tax exemption and the right to receive deductible contributions, which the report regards as the equivalent of a government subsidy. This premise is flawed in two important respects.

First, scholars and leaders in the sector believe that charities' public disclosure obligations derive from their fundamental nature as voluntary associations formed by private citizens to advance the public good, not from their receipt of favorable tax treatment. By definition, going back to their origins in English common law, charities are organized and operated for the benefit of the community. To qualify as a charity, an organization must dedicate all of its income and assets in perpetuity to serving the disadvantaged or otherwise providing goods and services for the benefit of the public at large. Charities were recognized as separate entities with legal rights and responsibilities long before there was a federal income tax code.

The need for disclosure stems from charities' unique social role. A charity must be transparent enough to make donors, volunteers, and partners confident that the charity will in fact advance public rather than private interests. This need for disclosure as a means of ensuring public trust is conceptually independent of the receipt of favorable tax treatment.

Second, any characterization of tax exemption and the charitable deduction as government subsidies and the view that the receipt of those subsidies creates a strong presumption in favor of increased disclosure is flawed. In this view, tax exemption and the charitable deduction are treated as tax benefits because they enable charities and their donors to avoid paying tax they would otherwise have to pay.

There have been years of serious academic debate over whether the charitable exemption and deduction are appropriately viewed as special benefits or as structural necessities of a properly calculated income tax. Legal experts on nonprofit law advise that a sound tax policy case can be made that neither the charitable tax exemption nor the charitable contribution deduction is properly characterized as government subsidies.

Furthermore, the logical extension of treating the charitable exemption and deduction as tax benefits would be to treat every deduction, credit, or exemption as a tax benefit. If we decide that the public has an interest in all tax benefits accorded under federal law, then disclosure should be required of all taxpayers who receive tax benefits in any form. Following this view, every taxable corporation with a business expense deduction or net operating loss carryover or every individual receiving a child care credit or mortgage interest deduction should also be required to disclose his or her tax returns.

Even the most ardent proponents of increased charity disclosure may not be prepared to adopt this general approach. We all recognize that confidentiality of tax return information is essential to fostering voluntary compliance with the system. Clearly, then, the receipt of tax benefits, whether in the form of the charitable exemption and deduction or the many benefits received by taxable entities and individuals, does not create a general presumption in favor of more disclosure.

Finally, even government entities funded entirely with public subsidies enjoy a significant zone of privacy. Clearly, Congress has recognized that even in the case of publicly funded governmental entities, where the case for public accountability is strongest, unlimited disclosure can be counterproductive. While INDEPENDENT SECTOR supports a high degree of transparency for charities, we believe it is extremely important to avoid reporting requirements that could have a chilling effect on charities' participation in the public policy process.

The nonprofit role in policy formulation

Because of their unique role in mobilizing citizens and communities to address issues of common concern, charities make an important and valuable contribution toward the development of public policy. Charities are on the front lines of the struggle against the most significant social problems, including hunger, poverty, discrimination, and disease, and are also the vanguard of many significant social innovations. The hands-on experience charities derive from their day-to-day work for the public good can help legislators at the national and state levels make more informed and enlightened decisions on the full range of issues that come before them. In Section 1307 of Public Law 94-455, the Tax Reform Act of 1976, which resulted in Internal Revenue Code Sections 4911 and 501(h), key members of Congress explicitly and repeatedly recognized the important contribution that charities make to the legislative process in the course of developing the landmark 1976 legislation clarifying and liberalizing the lobbying rules for public charities. The clear premise of this legislation, which should continue to guide Congress and the states, is that the public interest is served by encouraging more rather than less participation by charities in the public policy process.

As a practical matter, one of the chief barriers to such participation by charities in the public policy process is the complex set of federal and state rules governing lobbying by charities. Charities are subject not only to the federal tax law rules on lobbying but also to the federal Lobbying Disclosure Act, the separate lobbying restrictions related to the receipt of federal grant funds, and to various state lobby disclosure statutes. The regulations interpreting the federal tax limitations on lobbying alone total more than forty pages in the Code of Federal Regulations. The complexity of these rules has a substantial, and highly undesirable, chilling effect on participation in the democratic policymaking process for both smaller organizations with limited staff and access to legal counsel and larger organizations that must establish and maintain complex record-keeping systems.

Any additional reporting requirements could further deter charities from participating in the public policy process. This effect would be particularly troubling because charities are often the only parties able to speak on behalf of the least fortunate in our country. With the pervasive and corrupting influence of so much money in political campaigns at all levels of government, we have to ensure that charities can continue to speak for those without access to power. Serious consideration must be given to the effect that additional disclosure requirements can have on constitutional guarantees, including, most importantly, the effect on exercise of free speech.

Thus, absent a finding of an absolutely compelling public interest in additional disclosure, we should avoid imposing additional reporting burdens in this important and constitutionally sensitive area. None of the periodic proposals for increased disclosure has presented any evidence of abuses that needed to be addressed with respect to charities' participation in the policy formation process. In fact, observers have referred to such attempts as solutions in search of a problem.

Given the growing disaffection of many Americans from the public policy process, we should be doing everything possible to encourage, rather than discourage, active participation from all quarters of American society, including most especially the charities, in the public policy arena. And many Americans exercise their rights to participate as citizens through their nonprofit organizations.

The scope of the overall reporting obligations of charities should be determined through a careful cost-benefit analysis that weighs the public interests advanced by disclosure of particular information against those public interests undermined by additional disclosure. To be sure, there are important public interest issues that can be advanced by disclosure, such as:

- Increasing the public's ability to oversee tax-exempt organizations for the purpose of verifying that the organizations are serving the public and not private interests and are remaining faithful to the goals of their contributors and other supporters
- Increasing compliance with federal and state tax (and other applicable) laws
- Promoting the fair application and administration of the tax laws
- Encouraging giving, volunteerism, and collective action

However, it is not necessarily true that additional public disclosure necessarily increases public accountability. There is a nearly infinite amount of information that charities could be required to provide to the public. Substantially increased disclosure necessarily entails substantially increased costs. These are costs measured in the time and resources needed to learn about new legal requirements, change record-keeping systems, gather and store additional information, and deal with harassment from adversaries who use the required disclosure as an opportunity to distract the charity from its real work.

Time and resources spent on government paperwork are time and resources not spent on providing food, clothing, shelter, medical care, child care, and other vital services to the charity's beneficiaries. Governments should impose such administrative costs only when it is clear that they will produce a commensurate increase in meaningful public accountability.

Just as there are important public interests that may be advanced by disclosure, there are also important interests that may be adversely affected by increased mandatory disclosure—for example:

- Excessive reporting costs, which can drain resources from activities that further a charity's mission

- Onerous disclosure requirements, which can have the effect of compromising constitutionally protected rights to freedom of speech and freedom of association
- Privacy interests of donors, members, and other taxpayers whose personal information is in a charity's possession
- Ensuring competitive equality for unrelated business activities
- Promoting increased voluntary compliance and efficient tax administration
- Protecting appropriate privacy interests of exempt organizations in seeking determinations and rulings on proposed organizations and transactions

We cannot afford to underestimate the potentially negative effects of increased disclosure. In working to ensure appropriate transparency of charitable organizations, policymakers and regulators should recognize the very substantial amount of information that charities already disclose and give high priority to making this information more readily available to the public in user-friendly form.

The existing disclosure requirements that apply to charities under the federal tax law generate a substantial volume of publicly available information.[1] With the finalization of the regulations under Internal Revenue Code section 6104 in 2000, incentives are in place for more and more of that information to be readily available and easily searchable over the Internet.

Unfortunately, much of the most valuable information for the public is hidden among the more than four hundred separate pieces of data (not including attachments and schedules) that are found on the Internal Revenue Service's six-page Form 990. To illustrate, from the Form 990, any member of the public can already see the following information:

- Detailed description of activities furthering the charitable mission, including discussion of any significant changes in activities
- Total revenues

- Total expenses
- Names and addresses of all officers, directors, trustees, and key employees
- Compensation of officers and directors, trustees, and key employees
- Compensation of the five most highly paid employees other than officers, directors, or trustees

The list goes on, extensively, to provide much more information than the average citizen and even donor will want. Without an understandable users' guide, the public derives little benefit from much of the information already reported by charities. Recently, the Nonprofit Coordinating Committee of the City of New York has published Peter Swords' *How to Read the Form 990 & Find out What it Means*, which provides the interested reader with an introduction to the complexities of, and the valuable information contained within, nonprofits' annual information returns to the IRS (Swords, 2001).

Oversight of the charitable sector by both the government and the public could be dramatically improved by revising Form 990 so that it highlights critical information and facilitates the reader's understanding of the information and its significance. A top priority for the IRS in this regard should be providing, either directly or through nongovernmental intermediaries, on-line access to all Forms 990.

Technology and accountability

No discussion about nonprofits and accountability would be complete without some attention to the issues created by technology. With new capacities to give and solicit on-line, recruit volunteers and offer to volunteer, shop and thereby contribute to charity, and promote our causes on-line, it is only a matter of time before we begin to see errors, at the most benign, and outright fraud and abuse, at the worst. We—nonprofits, policymakers, and regulators—should be working together to develop guidelines, educate the public, and put in place reasonable policies that will facilitate all of this without placing undue burdens on the organizations doing the work for the public good. The National Association of State Charity Officials developed and disseminated for comment the Charleston Principles, which make a good contribution toward beginning to address the potential problems with the increased use of technology and the absence of regulatory or oversight mechanisms, or even standards of practice or codes of ethics (see Chapter Six).

Conclusion

It bears repeating that most of the leadership of the philanthropic-nonprofit sector is committed to the highest standards of accountability, openness, and disclosure. We recognize that if we lose the public trust, we lose our ability to serve the public good. We understand that there is a need for policies, legislation, regulation, and oversight. But we will resist any attempts that will increase the burden and costs to nonprofits without an evident and compelling benefit to the public. We will also oppose with every tool at our disposal any attempts to curb the advocacy rights of nonprofits and infringe on their rights of free speech and association.

Note

1. The existing disclosure requirements that apply to charities under the Federal tax law generate a substantial volume of publicly available information. All charities are required by section 6104(d) of the Internal Revenue Code (26 U.S.C. § 6104(d)) to provide copies of their three most recent IRS returns (Form 990) to any person who asks for them. Charities are also required to provide copies of their IRS exemption applications (Form 1023) on request. Charities have an incentive to place these documents on the Internet, as regulation section 301.6104(d)-2 (26 C.F.R. § 301.6104(d)-2) provides that if they do so, and direct any person asking for a copy to the appropriate web address, they are not required to provide photocopies of these documents.

References

INDEPENDENT SECTOR. *Facts and Findings: Taking the Pulse of Americans' Attitudes Toward Charities*. Washington, D.C.: 2001a, 1–3.

INDEPENDENT SECTOR. *Giving and Volunteering in the United States: Key Findings*. Washington, D.C.: 2001b.

INDEPENDENT SECTOR. *The New Nonprofit Almanac in Brief*. Washington, D.C.: 2001c.

Swords, P. *How to Read the Form 990 & Find Out What it Means*. New York: Nonprofit Coordinating Committee for the City of New York, 2001.

U.S. Congress. Joint Committee on Taxation. *Overview of Present-Law Rules and Description of Certain Proposals Relating to Disclosure of Information by Tax-Exempt Organizations with Respect to Political Activities (Report JCX-59-00)*. June 19, 2000.

SARA E. MELENDÉZ *is president and chief executive officer of* *INDEPENDENT SECTOR*.

Conclusion

THE RESOURCES committed to public benefit by nongovernmental organizations in the United States are enormous, yet they are dwarfed by the needs. Holding even a small part of those assets, expending some fraction of those revenues, entails a clearly important responsibility. Yet the dimensions of that responsibility cannot fully be defined.

The special characteristics of the work that nonprofits do complicate the issue further. Many nonprofits produce classic public goods, for which the producer cannot insist on compensation from every beneficiary. (The advocacy work for which nonprofits are justly admired is a powerful case in point.) Further, acting as an agent for donors' good intentions involves an inherent tension between satisfying their personal interests and achieving the wider goals that depend on their support. Similarly, the preferential tax treatments accorded nonprofits' operations may encourage displacement of resources, especially the resource of management attention, into activities with tangential (at best) connections to the underlying purposes on which the favorable tax status depends. These and other aspects of "nonprofitness" are present to a greater or lesser degree in the daily routines of people who work for, manage, and lead charitable organizations in the United States. Steering a responsible course through these conflicting currents will never be easy, and success will never be assured.

Among the aids to navigation that have been developed in response to the inescapable tensions present under these conditions are the mechanisms of accountability described by the authors of the chapters in this issue. As their discussions make clear, it is unreasonable to hope that access to information about nonprofits' resources and activities can completely prevent abuses and disappointments. Reading these chapters also makes clear, though, that accountability in this sense is key to maintaining a strong and effective nonprofit sector.

Many discussions of accountability, including those in this issue, emphasize its importance to maintaining public confidence in and financial support for the work of nonprofit organizations. Before leaving the topic, it is appropriate to turn the mirror around briefly and ask about the accountability of donors, regulators, and policymakers and the effects of the ways they do their work on the effectiveness of the nonprofit sector. Are donors ready to accept the facts of life represented by overhead and fundraising costs? Can regulators and watchdogs articulate how their work ensures appropriate uses of charitable resources without unnecessarily distracting energies from the important tasks nonprofits exist to perform? Do funding agencies—both major private donors and government units whose programs operate through support for nonprofits—assure themselves and the wider public that the procedures they follow in awarding and monitoring grants are tuned to minimize any expense unrelated to accomplishing their goals? The disclosure of data about operations and the tools for assessing outcomes that have been, rightly, urged on direct service and advocacy organizations can surely be adapted to answering these and related questions as well.

Statistics (largely based on accountability documents) demonstrate rapid growth in both the size and the complexity of America's nonprofit sector. Nothing about those trends makes nonprofits' obedience to the unenforceable any easier. Continuing the effort to strengthen the effectiveness not only of America's nonprofits but also of accountability itself is a task worthy of the energies of people who care about the nonprofit sector and its work.

Putnam Barber
Editor

PUTNAM BARBER *is president of The Evergreen State Society in Seattle, Washington, and editor of the Internet Nonprofit Center.*

Index

Back Issue/Subscription Order Form

Copy or detach and send to:
Jossey-Bass, 989 Market Street, San Francisco, CA 94103-1741

Call or fax toll free!
Phone 888-378-2537 6AM-5PM PST; Fax 800-605-2665

Back issues: Please send me the following issues at $28 each
(Important: please include series initials and issue number, such as PF10)

1. PF ____

____

____

$ __________ Total for single issues

$ __________ Shipping charges (for single issues ***only;*** subscriptions are exempt from shipping charges): Up to $30, add $\$5^{50}$ • $\$30^{01}$–$50, add $\$6^{50}$
$\$50^{01}$–$75, add $8 • $\$75^{01}$–$100, add $10 • $\$100^{01}$–$150, add $12
Over $150, call for shipping charge

Subscriptions Please ❑ start ❑ renew my subscription to *New Directions for Philanthropic Fundraising* at the following rate:

US:	❑ Individual $75	❑ Institutional $147
Canada:	❑ Individual $75	❑ Institutional $187
All others:	❑ Individual $99	❑ Institutional $221

NOTE: Issues are published quarterly. Subscriptions are for the calendar year only. Subscriptions begin with the Spring issue. Add appropriate sales tax for your state for single issue orders. No sales tax for U.S. subscriptions.

$ __________ Total single issues and subscriptions (Canadian residents, add GST for subscriptions and single issues)

❑ Payment enclosed (U.S. check or money order only)

❑ VISA, MC, AmEx, Discover Card #__________________ Exp. date________

Signature ________________________ Day phone ______________

❑ Bill me (U.S. institutional orders only. Purchase order required)

Purchase order #____

Federal Tax ID 135593032 GST 89102-8052

Name ____

Address ____

____

Phone______________________ E-mail __________________

For more information about Jossey-Bass, visit our Web site at:
www.josseybass.com **PRIORITY CODE = ND1**

Previous Issues Available

NEW DIRECTIONS FOR PHILANTHROPIC FUNDRAISING

PF30 The Role of the Planned Giving Professional: Serving Nonprofit Organizations and Their Donors, *Gordon D. Chavers*

PF29 Understanding the Needs of Donors: The Supply Side of Charitable Giving, *Eugene R. Tempel, Dwight F. Burlingame*

PF28 Approaching Foundations: Suggestions and Insights for Fundraisers, *Sandra A. Glass*

PF27 Serving the Public Trust: Insights into Fundraising Research and Practice (Volume 2), *Paul P. Pribbenow*

PF26 Serving the Public Trust: Insights into Fundraising Research and Practice (Volume 1), *Paul P. Pribbenow*

PF25 The Impact of Technology on Fundraising, *Dwight F. Burlingame, Michael J. Poston*

PF24 Hispanic Philanthropy: Exploring the Factors That Influence Giving and Asking, *Lilya Wagner, Allan Figueroa Deck*

PF23 The Changing World of Foundation Fundraising: New Challenges and Opportunities, *Sandra A. Glass*

PF22 Understanding and Improving the Language of Fundraising, *Timothy L. Seiler*

PF21 Capital Campaigns: Realizing Their Power and Potential, *Andrea Kihlstedt, Robert Pierpont*

PF20 Small Nonprofits: Strategies for Fundraising Success, *Mary Louise Mussoline*

PF19 Women as Fundraisers: Their Experience in and Influence on an Emerging Profession, *Julie C. Conry*

PF18 Marketing the Nonprofit: The Challenge of Fundraising in a Consumer Culture, *Margaret M. Maxwell*

PF17 The Practice of Stewardship in Religious Fundraising, *Daniel Conway, Cecelia Hart Price*

PF16 Developing Major Gifts, *Dwight F. Burlingame, James M. Hodge*

PF15 The Professionalization of Fundraising: Implications for Education, Practice, and Accountability, *Eugene R. Tempel, Sara B. Cobb, Warren F. Ilchman*